BLINDNESS SHOULD NOT BE A BURDEN

Archie R. Silago

Blindness Should Not Be a Burden
Archie Silago

ISBN 978-1-935089-31-5

Published by
Acacia Publishing, Inc.
www.acaciapublishing.com

Printed and Bound in the United States of America

Acknowledgments

There are many people I wish to thank who are family and friends as they had significant influence in my life.

First I want to thank my mother, Rosie Ashley, and my late father, Jake Silago Sr., my sisters Etta, Cynthia, Jolene and late sister Gracie., my brothers Jerry, Steve and Jake Jr. My nieces Shawmarie, Jerrileen, Yvonne, Karleen, Jackie, Stephanie, Becky and others. My nephews Eugene, Stacey, Jon/ty, Jackson, Steven and others. My grandchildren Rylee, Kylee, Ty/Jordan and others.My sisters in-law Bessie, Alberta and Ruth. I owe special thanks to all my immediate family for being there for me when I really needed someone. Life without them would have been almost impossible. At the beginning, living in a world of total physical darkness was unpredictable and very difficult.

Next I wish to thank my friends for their support and encouragement. They include Lew Manas, Angela Kyle, Leoda Garcia and Kelly Burma of the Commission for the Blind program. John and Helen Ridley. Alamogordo, NM. Nancy and Tina April, Cloudcroft, NM. Louisianna McDonald, Las Cruces, NM, Allen Riley, Harry Lujan and others with the American Indian Program, NMSU, Las Cruces, NM, and the late Dr. Robert Keenan, Gallup, NM.

Finally, I wish to give special thanks to Karen Gray, President of Acacia Publishing, Incorporated for believing in me and getting my project to become reality. This includes the rest of the staff at Acacia Publishing Incorporated for the roles they played

Chapter One
Birthplace And Childhood

I was born in the early 1950s in the small town of Crownpoint, New Mexico, on the Navajo reservation in northwest New Mexico. The population was probably around 1,000 people, mostly Native Americans. I was born into a family of five – my parents, Rita and Jack Sr., two sisters, Etta and Gracie, and a brother, Jerry. Two new brothers, Steve and Jake Jr., joined the family later on. I had to look after these two little guys. For example, if someone made them cry or got them in trouble I looked into their situation. The majority of the time it was some kid older than they who picked on them.

While growing up there, I went hiking and camping on top of the mesas that bordered Crownpoint. Sometimes at night during a camping trip I looked down at Crownpoint from one of the ledges. Many times I camped out overnight or even for a whole week with friends. I took canned meat, canned fruits, bread or crackers to eat. Sometimes a couple of the older boys who had money hiked back to town. When they returned they brought hamburger meat and hot dogs to cook over the camp fire.

Satan's Pass, Crownpoint, NM

One night after enjoying some hamburgers and hot dogs, we were sitting around the camp fire telling phony ghost stories. All of a sudden a strange noise silenced the group. One of the older boys, Phil, whispered, "Stay quiet, boys," and slowly stood up. We all sat still, looking at one another, listening. Again whispering, he said, "Hand me the rifle" and shot a few rounds into the air. Right after the shots were fired we heard something run off into the woods away from camp.

He sat back down and stated with self-assurance, "Okay, boys, now you can get some sleep. Don't be scared." Another boy, Ted, mumbled, "What do you think that noise was?"

Phil replied, "It was probably nothing."

Just then another boy, Frank, teasingly said, "It was probably a skin walker checking on us," then laughed. The next morning one of the boys, George, still concerned said, "I looked around everywhere but did not see anything crazy."

I hiked and explored the majority of these mesas as far as five miles from town. Several of us boys carved our initials on the rock formation and the carvings may still be there. I never went back up there after moving away from Crownpoint. We spent a good amount of time on these mesas whatever the season was. I remember building small huts out of evergreen bushes to keep ourselves warm, especially during Christmas break. There were many times I went with my three brothers Jerry, Steve, and Jake Jr. We took potatoes, lard, chili peppers, bacon, canned meat or canned beans. Our older brother, Jerry, would mix some of this food and cook a good meal over a campfire. He took good care of us while we were out there.

I hunted for shark's teeth and fossils that were embedded in the sandstone formation. I learned this from members of a church group that came to town during the summer months. I enjoyed making new friends when they came to town. Each summer there was a different group of people. I think they were college age young adults. They helped when we had our summer recreation or vacation Bible school. I enjoyed being with these individuals because they liked the outdoors. Cold watermelon and soda pop were my favorite treats served at these activities that I enjoyed with everyone.

We always had a good time and everyone laughed

and enjoyed themselves. During the evening, we watched a movie or tried to learn how to dance to music coming from the jukebox. These individuals came from different parts of the country to experience life on the reservation. I remember that one of the volunteers came all the way from Hawaii. He always liked to dance and talk about the beaches. We decided to nickname him Beach Boy.

The church groups that volunteered to come to Crownpoint acknowledged, "We don't regret coming here." The place where these new friends stayed was with local church members.

One of the groups planted a watermelon patch while staying in Crownpoint. When the watermelons were ripe they turned out to be sweet and juicy ones. One day I got together with some of my friends with a crazy idea.

I suggested, "Let's go over to the watermelon patch tonight."

One of the boys, Ted, responded, "What for? Are you crazy?"

I asked, "Who wants to steal a watermelon tonight to munch down?" Some of the boys agreed to go. When it got dark enough we started toward the watermelon patch.

One little kid, Bruce, whispered with a squeaky voice, "I'm scared but I want to eat some watermelon."

I replied, "If you're scared just get out of here and don't tell anybody what we're doing."

Approaching the fence, Ted instructed, "Wait right there; I think there is someone standing outside the house."

I quickly said, "Hurry, lie down on the ground before he sees us."

Just then that little kid, Bruce, came toward us, crying. He mumbled, "I am scared of the dark."

"Shut up before somebody hears you! Come and lie down over here," I ordered.

He whispered, "Okay," trying to stop crying.

I asked, "Is the coast clear now?"

One of the boys, Tim, slowly stood up and answered, "Yes, I don't see anybody outside the house." We had him keeping watch for us just in case someone came along.

I said, "Okay, boys, let's get our watermelon."

Ted added, "Yeah, hurry up, slowpokes."

I quickly asked, "Who wants to climb over the fence with me?"

"I'll go with you," Ted responded.

I instructed two boys, Rob and Jeff, "Wait right here by the fence; we will give you the watermelon."

They stood near the fence, ready to go. I said, "Find one close to the fence."

My partner Ted replied, "Okay" just as he stumbled over a watermelon. Then he said, "Hey, buddy, here is a good one."

"Where? Let me see."

"Right under your big nose."

"Good; let's take this one." I grabbed the watermelon but it was slippery. "Hey, buddy, help me carry it to the fence." We took a good hold and carried it to the fence.

I instructed, "Here you are. Rob and Jeff, take it under the bridge and wait there."

They answered, "Okay," taking the melon with them.

"Hey, buddy, do you think we should take another

one?" I asked.

Ted quickly replied, "No, one is good enough for tonight."

"Okay, buddy," I responded.

"Come on, what are you doing over there?" He asked.

I answered, "Checking out these watermelons. There are some pretty big ones."

"Hurry up, let's go before we get caught," he said.

"We won't get caught. Remember, that crybaby Bruce left."

"The church people will probably serve some tomorrow," Ted commented.

I said, "Okay, let's go," and climbed over the fence.

"Hurry up! What is your problem?" Ted asked.

I asked, "What do you think those boys are doing with the watermelon?"

He responded, "They'd better not start eating it without us," then laughed.

After getting a little ways from the watermelon patch we started running toward the bridge. Just as we ducked under, a car passed by that seem to slow down. Puffing, I muttered, "I hope that was not a cop."

"We should go somewhere else to eat this melon." Jeff said.

I answered, "That's right. It might have been a cop."

Just then, Rob quickly intervened. "Wait up; let me go up and check." He took off climbing up the hill and looked around quickly. He returned and confirmed, "The coast is clear. Let me have some watermelon," then giggled.

I motioned, "Okay, boys break it open. Let's have some of this good watermelon."

We dropped the watermelon on a large flat rock to break it open. Ted had a pocket knife and he managed to cut some of it into small pieces. The watermelon tasted good – it was sweet and juicy. We sat there under the bridge for a while, full of watermelon. Every now and then a car passing over the bridge made it vibrate a little.

Apprehensively I muttered, "I don't know if any of you feels bad after doing this." Ted boldly replied, "What do you mean feel bad? Remember, you were the one who wanted to steal the watermelon."

I replied, "I don't know; maybe it's because our new friends are the ones who planted the watermelon patch."

Jeff responded, "It's just too bad. Here, eat some more," and handed me a piece.

Just then that little kid, Bruce, with the squeaky voice whined, "I want to go home."

I responded "Go ahead, we're not holding on to you."

He said, "Somebody take me home; I'm scared of the dark."

"Can one of you take him home?" I asked.

Rob replied, "Yeah, before he starts crying again like a little girl."

Bruce retorted, "I am not a little girl."

It seemed like during the summer months the rain was almost frequent. I guess it was the monsoon season – as kids neither we knew nor even cared. Just about mid-morning there would be a puff of cloud in the southern skies over the mesas. Later the clouds would increase in size, then become rain clouds.

The dirt roads and unpaved streets always got muddy. There was an arroyo that came from the base of the mesas and ran through the middle of town out into the flats beyond town. I enjoyed the rainfall and the rushing water that made its way down the arroyo. Before the rainwater came rushing down, some of us boys started gathering logs and old lumber. We placed them alongside the arroyo to throw in when the arroyo filled with rainwater.

We ran along the arroyo to see what would happen to the logs and lumber, especially when they reached a 30 foot drop in a small canyon of rock formation. I can still see the rushing water spinning rapidly at the bottom of this waterfall. Reaching this point, most of the logs and lumber broke apart and disappeared down the arroyo. I never knew where the arroyo went or where it ended.

By that time our clothes and tennis shoes were pretty dirty with mud. We would be all tired from what was fun to us. Trying to clean up, one of the boys, George, said, "Okay, let's get out of here before someone's dad gets mad at us."

I answered, "That's right. I don't want to get in trouble because these little boys got all dirty."

Large trees which grew on both sides of the arroyo made playing more fun. I remember the tree house I helped build with the boys. Many times during the summer nights we hid there from the night watchman, Mr. Lincoln, and others. Teasing the night watchman would upset him, and he would come after us. One time he firmly stated, "When I get a hold of one of you boys I will take you to the police."

One boy, Rob bravely replied, "Go ahead try it; you are too slow, so how can you catch us?"

Mr. Lincoln said, "I am tired of you guys always picking on me; you should pick on someone else."

One of the little guys, Frank, fearfully suggested, "Let's get out of here before he really catches one of us."

"Yeah, he might be calling the police right now," I added.

Another frightened little boy, Sammy, chimed in, "What do you think he will do with us if he catches us?"

Jeff, responded, "He will probably take you to the police or spank you, and then take you home."

Sometimes I brought canned food I took from home and an old blanket to spend the night in the tree house with the boys. When we all got there, Albert would say, "Okay boys, what did you bring to eat? I'm hungry."

I responded, "Some canned meat and canned beans. What about you?"

He replied boldly, "I am the leader; I don't have to bring anything."

Another boy, John, retorted, "What do you mean, leader? You're supposed to bring something just like the rest of us."

Another boy, Paul, quickly intervened, "Come on, guys, just eat what we have. If you don't like it then just beat it." We usually shared whatever we brought, then spent the night. We made the tree house with a lock on the door. The older boys were the ones who kept other kids away from here.

Many times the tree house served as a military fort when we played our army games. After setting up in our fort, I looked at my friend Melvin and asked, "Did you bring your machine gun?"

He replied, "Yes, I did."

"Let me see it," I demanded. Some of my friends were pretty talented when it came to making their wooden machine guns.

"No, I am not going to let you use it, because the last time you messed it up." Just then George said, "Hey, do we have enough dirt clods for our hand grenades?"

I answered, "They are stacked in that box in the corner." We actually threw dirt clods at each other until someone started crying. We picked up a lot of ideas from watching war movies – like taking a tree limb with a bunch of leaves on it and using it for a helmet. We also adopted the use of foxholes the same way. I remember after watching a war movie we would pretend to be one of the heroes in the movie. Another homemade gadget was a rubber band gun. We used these gadgets to kill little bugs, and unknowingly sharpened our marksmanship.

Getting away from the gang with one of my friends, Donald, we went to his house to play army. We played with his toys – a complete army set. They were plastic army men, jeeps, trucks, tanks and flags. We would set up our men and equipment on each side. Using a rubber band gun, we took turns shooting at each other's setup. The winner was declared after someone knocked out everything on one side.

Another fun activity during my childhood was

swimming in the rainwater pond. One day around mid-morning I saw one of my friends, Ray, near the house goofing around.

Sitting on the porch, I looked at him, asking, "Hey, dude, are you lost?"

He replied, "No, what's up with you?"

I asked, "What brings you here?"

He said, "Hey, dude, do you feel like swimming in the pond today?"

"I don't know, what about you?"

"Do you think the other boys want to go?"

"I don't know, why don't you ask them yourself?"

He said, "Can you ask them for me?"

"We can both ask them but remember, one of their mothers does not like it when we ask them to go."

"I think they're just a bunch of chickens or just plain scared."

"Let's just go by ourselves," I suggested.

"I guess we can do that."

"Maybe we can throw in the raft to float around."

Unsatisfied Ray stated, "I am going to ask them anyway."

"Go ahead. Watch what their mother will say."

After all this, the two of us went swimming alone. A few of the boys came over later to join us. I swam around for a while and then got out to lie on the raft.

After getting out of the water, when it dried off I could feel the sand on my skin. One of the boys, Bill, who came later, asked, "Does any one want some of this chewing tobacco?"

I answered, "Yes, I'll try some – let me have it."

"Are you sure? It could make you sick."

"If that stuff will get me sick, why do you chew it?"

"It makes me tough," he bragged, then laughed.

When the girls would see us after we went swimming, they would laugh about us. I remember Vicky said, "You boys are a bunch of crazy guys, swimming in that muddy water."

Ray responded, "Go home play with your dolls or make some mud pies," then laughed.

She replies, "I'll make some mud pies – then you can eat them."

Another boy, Melvin, said, "Come on, dude, leave your girlfriend alone," then giggled.

Located in the downtown area of Crownpoint, the Campus was a special place to many, both young and old,. It was a large area covered with green grass and large trees. At the north end was a fairly large garden with different kinds of pretty flowers.

Running along the outskirts of campus were nicely trimmed hedges parallel with a sidewalk. The oval-shaped park was well maintained. At the south end stood several brick buildings which were the government boarding school where many Navajo children lived while they attended school. They came from different areas through out the eastern agency. I made friends with the ones I attended classes with at the elementary school.

The government offices and the superintendent's house were located at the north end. Each office building and large house was surrounded by green grass and large trees.

The outskirts of campus where the sidewalk ran were a favorite for many. People went walking there during the cool summer evenings. When the boarding school was close for the summer with hardly anyone around, some of the boys and girls would ride their bikes on the oval-shaped sidewalk.

Other times some of the boys would race their bikes here. I did not have a bike of my own but I rode one when one of my friends, John, let me use his.

Before riding one day he asked, "Hey, dude, do you want to learn how to ride a bike?"

"Yes, but you have a big bike," I said.

"Yeah, but don't be afraid. I will guard you all the time."

All excited, I replied, "Okay, buddy."

"I'll hold the bike still while you get on."

I said, "Okay. Please don't let me fall."

He laughed, then confirmed, "I won't let you fall, little buddy."

I courageously replied, "Okay," and then climbed onto the bike.

He gave me a good push then said, "Pedal the bike hard and keep the handle bars straight." I could hear him running after me as I pedaled down the unpaved street. He shouted out, "I think you are getting the hang of it." He caught up with me as I attempted to make my stop.

After stopping he held the bike steady so I could get off.

"Boy, that was fun," I said.

"You did a good job. If we keep this up you will learn how to ride by yourself."

Excited I said, "Man, I really rode a big bike, huh?"

"Yes, you sure did," he said, smiling.

I kept saying, "I still can't believe it."

"Soon you will learn how to start and stop without any help," he said.

Eventually, I learned how to ride any size bike with the help of my friend John. He was one of the older boys who did a lot for us younger ones.

Another game I liked to play at campus was "chicken fight." Here, we teamed up with one of the older boys, riding piggyback on him. We tried to pull our opponents off of their partner's back without falling from ours. When it was time, one of the older boys would say, "Okay, boys, get your partners." I teamed up with Tony and talked about how we were going to do the chicken fight.

He explained, "Okay, buddy, I want you to hold onto my shirt real tight with one hand."

I replied, "Okay, real tight, I got it."

Then he added, "With your other hand I want you to grab that kid by the shirt; then we will drag him off." There were several teams and sometimes even the girls joined in on this rough game. Some of these girls were pretty tough and kept up with some of us boys.

My partner Tony said, "Okay, buddy, It's our turn. All you have to do is remember what I told you."

I eagerly replied, "Yeah, grab that kid by the shirt and drag him off." Between the other team and ours, we both struggled, trying to pull each other off. Finally I got pulled off and eliminated.

Tony said, "That's okay, buddy, we will get them the next time." This went on for some time until a winner was declared.

Another game I like playing on the grass was having a kid's rodeo. The older boys pretended to be bucking broncos by jumping around with a kid on their back. They wrapped a rope around the older boy's chest area that the smaller kid could hold onto. Sometimes, Ray would let the rider wear his cowboy hat. If we wanted to try staying aboard one of these wild guys we paid a dime for entry fee. It was not easy trying to stay aboard, especially when the boy started spinning around then suddenly stopped. I remember several times I hit the grass pretty hard on my back and actually felt it.

Away from the campus area among some pinon trees, the older boys made a bucking barrel with a 55 gallon drum. There were three cables connected to the barrel, with one up front and two in the back. The cables were connected to three different pinon trees. The way this bucking barrel operated was using manpower. Three boys pulled and jerked the cables as hard as they could. This made the barrel bounce around like a bucking bronco. They pulled and jerked vigorously for about ten seconds. It did not take long for some of the riders to be dismounted.

This added some real life-like drama to our wild rodeos. There was a rope wrapped around the barrel for the rider to hold onto. The barrel was padded underneath where we held onto the rope. Trying to stay aboard one of these barrels took practice. It was always fun and when the riders got bucked off they landed on some soft sand. We made these rodeo games as real as possible, enjoying the adrenalin rush they gave us.

Most of the games we played we used our imagination or handmade toys and still had fun. I think we learned some of those things – both good and bad – from the older boys we hung out with. I think the older boys enjoyed it as much as we did. I remember some of them hardly complained. After a day of messing and goofing around with them, sometimes they treated us younger boys to a soda pop that cost a dime back then.

Another wild and daring experience was being at a squaw dance, a traditional Navajo traditional ceremony performed during the summer months. They usually started on Thursday night and lasted until the crack of dawn of the following Monday morning. For us boys, Friday or Saturday night was the perfect time to go there if it was near Crownpoint.

After supper on Friday or Saturday evening we would meet at one of our hideouts. Goofing around at the hideout, one of the older boys, Paul, would say, "Hey, boys, who wants to check out the squaw dance tonight?"

Some of the boys would respond, "I want to go." I would go along just to goof around.

Paul would ask, "Are you sure you want to go? You might be too small, little boy."

Once, one of the boys, Melvin, said, "I took one of my dad's cigarettes."

Paul asked, "Who all has some money with them?" Most of the boys would have a few coins in their pockets. We would walk up the hill on the dirt road that led out of town to hitchhike. We would split up into a couple of groups and wait at different places along the road to catch a ride. The plan was to meet up at the squaw dance after getting there.

George coached, "Listen, when I say 'now' you guys start waving down the driver."

Another boy, Ray, added, "When they stop, tell the

driver we need a ride to the squaw dance." We could usually catch a ride in back of a pickup truck. Sometimes we would catch a ride with one of the boys' parents. I liked riding in back of those trucks where you could stare at the night sky. I remember that Crownpoint had one of the clearest night skies and you could see millions of bright stars. I also remember one time when looking at the night sky I saw a small dot of light moving across the sky; I wondered if it was a satellite.

Once we got to the squaw dance we would look around to see if there was anybody we knew. Melvin, with the cigarettes and chewing tobacco, generously said, "Here you go, boys, have some of this if you want." It was nighttime with a bunch of campfires burning that provided some of the lighting. Some families would have a concession stand selling fry bread and soda pop. They used a gas lantern for lighting so there was not much lighting around there. Walking around there at night we had to be careful. Several people rode their horses there as part of the tradition. If you were not careful you could easily bump into one of those horses standing in the dark.

There was always someone at these squaw dances selling beer or wine. One of the older boys, Ray, asked, "Do you boys want to get some beer or wine to try?"

Tony, standing next to him, responded, "What do you mean, beer or wine to try? Where can we get it?"

I volunteered, "I think Jimmy's dad might be selling some."

Then Tony replied, "Hey, since you know this kid, maybe you can ask his dad."

I said, "I don't know but I can try."

"What do you mean, try? Are you chicken, or what?"

"No, I am not chicken; all I need is some money and one of you guys to go with me."

Standing there, we all pitched in some money and decided to try and get a couple bottles of wine. Taking the money, we walked over to a car parked in the dark with very little lighting. I approached this one kid I sort of knew and courageously asked, "Hey, is your dad selling any beer or wine?"

Jimmy quickly replied, "Yeah, but I don't think he will sell you any because you guys are too little."

We left and I suggested, "Hey, buddy, we need to find an older man who might help us get the stuff."

Ray responded, "Let me ask that man standing over there since I can speak some Navajo."

I agreed, "Okay, go ahead give it a try." He managed to get the man, Lee, to purchase a couple of bottles.

With Lee following us, my buddy said, "I promised this guy some money or a drink."

I asked, "So what did he decide to do?"

He answered, "He wants to drink some."

After taking a drink, Lee said, "If you boys want to get some more I will get it for you." We passed the bottle around and those of us who wanted some, drank some.

After drinking some of this wild- tasting wine I asked, "How do you boys feel?"

Ray responded, "It feels like there is a warm fire in my tummy," then giggled.

Tony had a pack of chewing gum that he offered to us. He said, "Have some gum to kill the smell of that wild tasting wine."

Tony ended up getting sick and vomited next to some bushes. The wine did something to the rest of us that made us feel funny. I noticed that the only way to drink this stuff was real fast. That way most of us missed the awful taste.

I really did not understand the purpose for having the squaw dances. It seemed like it was a good time to be crazy and have some fun. I hung out all night with my buddies I came with. Eventually, I found a place to crash out in back of a friend's pickup truck. Sometimes we huddled up together alongside of someone's camp fire.

The next morning was always a good treat for everyone. There was a place where people gathered under a shade hut made of logs and oak brush. Standing there among the people, Navajo men sang traditional songs related to the squaw dance.

During this time some other people brought a bunch of goodies that they tossed into the crowd. The more these Navajo men sang, the more goodies were tossed out for them. I grabbed some of these goodies with my buddies – goodies like cracker jacks, popcorn balls, candy bars, chewing gum, soda pop and others. We managed to grab enough for us guys to enjoy, then started thinking about home. When I got home it seemed like I could still hear the Navajo men singing somewhere off in the distance. Mother already had a good idea where I was the night before. Anyone could smell camp fire smoke on my clothes, even from a mile away. One thing that she did not know about us was the drinking wine, smoking, and chewing tobacco.

During the winter time when it snowed in Crownpoint the snow stayed with us for several weeks. We were able to go snow sledding, make snowmen and have snowball fights. One event I recall that was special to me about the good old winters of Crownpoint involved an igloo. My brothers Jerry and Steve and I with a couple of friends, John and Tony, built an igloo out of snow. We got some cardboard boxes that were the same size. We compacted snow into the boxes to make snow blocks. We placed the snow blocks in a row, stacking them on top of each other just like building a wall. The igloo stood up for several days. The freezing cold nights helped the igloo stay up longer. I remember some people visiting relatives from out of town who took pictures of the igloo.

The long slanted hillsides beneath the mesas made a perfect place to go snow sledding. I went there with the other kids using tire tubes or sleds. Only a few kids were able to have nice sleds that were bought from the neighboring towns. Dad made us boys a homemade sled out of lumber and painted it red. For some reason, the homemade sled at different times outran the store-bought ones. Some of the girls and boys liked our little sled. They wanted to try it so my older brother Jerry let them. Some of the boys did not like our homemade sled so they teased us about it. Sometimes we got into an argument with these boys and some of the kids backed us up. My brothers and I always looked out for one another because of how we were treated growing up. For example, if something bad happened in town we were already accused.

These are some of the memorable events that took place in my life growing up in Crownpoint before the family moved when I turned 12. Two of my brothers, Jerry and Jake Jr., later returned to Crownpoint to work and live. Some of my childhood friends decided to remain there to make a living. Sometimes I cross paths with these girls or boys here and there. When we do we always talk about the good old days of Crownpoint when we were kids. Unfortunately, some of my other childhood friends died an early death for one reason or another.

Chapter Two
Houses I Lived In

Growing up in Crownpoint I remember that my family lived in four different houses. Each house we lived in was probably a governmental unit. The fact that Mother worked at the hospital during this time made her eligible to rent. The first place I remember living was in an elongated wooden building. Several families lived there as this building was sectioned off so that each family had a living room, bedroom and a kitchen area. Each section had a small front porch with steps. I remember this because my friend Rob and I would sit under the porch in the shade.

One morning mother shouted across the room, "What time is it?"

I confidently replied, "It is a quarter to seven."

She responded, "Okay," and then left for work. The way I did this was by comparing 25 minutes to 25 cents. The fact that a quarter before or after met 15 minutes instead of 25 minutes was something I learned later. I hardly remember what my sisters Etta and Gracie and older brother Jerry did when we lived there. I remember a little of what I did with Mother, Dad and my little buddies.

One day Shorty, the next door neighbor, came over to talk with Dad. He said, "Hey, partner, we are moving out so you can cut a doorway in the wall." Dad answered, "A doorway, what for?"

Shorty said, "That way you can use both units and have more room." Later that day Dad decided to cut a doorway through the wall that divided our sections.

My friends and I liked playing in this little orange brick building next to where we lived. This brick building was where coal was stored for the families' winter heating use. I remember this place well because we kids liked playing in the shining black coal.

I think it was the sound of the coal crackling we liked when we jumped on it. My two friends, Rob and John, who lived a couple of sections down from us, and I went there all the time. After spending a good amount of time in the coal we went home all dirty and hungry. When we got home we got scolded for getting our clothes dirty or torn. I guess this was because we lived in hard times in our family's life, something we would have never understood as kids back then.

I remember playing in the landscape of wild bushes and trees behind our long building. The stems on these bushes made perfect arrows as they were long and straight. There was another bush that had thicker stems that we used to make bows. Between both bushes, we could make a complete bow and arrow set. The sets were not the best but for playing cowboys and Indians but they did the trick. Other homemade items were the slingshots we made from Y shaped tree branches and strips of tire tubes. I recall that only the older boys carried a sling shot and little round rocks with them. If one of the mothers was looking for her kid, usually these bushes or under someone's porch were the places to look,.

As time went on, we eventually moved to another house as did everyone there. Not too long after leaving what was home to many of us, some workmen came in to tear down everything in sight. New trailer-like homes that were individually fenced in changed the scenery. Nearby, a large garage was built to work on large trucks and tractors. I remember this place because I could smell gasoline, diesel fuel and grease. I can still see the men who worked there with the oil and grease spots on their work clothes. I liked going there to watch these guys work. Sometimes one of the workers would give a us a soda pop and tell us to share it.

The second house the family lived in was a yellow one with white trim. It was located just below the hospital where Mother worked. This trailer-like house had wooden floors. I remember the floors well because we helped our sisters Etta and Gracie shine them up. The way we helped was that our sisters would have one or two of us sit on a soft cotton blanket. They would then pull the blanket throughout the house with us sitting on it. Doing this gave the floor a nice shine. Here I noticed more about being with my sisters and brothers and than in the last house.

Life seemed to be a lot better for my family as both parents worked. Mother continued her work in the kitchen at the hospital. I can still remember the uniform she wore to work. Dad worked for the government as a truck driver. Sometimes he had to park his rig in back of the house. He did this because he was leaving early the next morning. For me, just looking at that huge truck gave me a scary feeling. I kept thinking that if I got to close to it the truck would start up and run over me. One day my older brother Jerry took me to the truck so I would not be afraid of it anymore. Sometimes dad took him along on his long road trip. Mother packed him a separate lunch that probably made him feel like a worker. I started feeling sad when I heard that truck start up the road that led out of town in the morning. I would wait around for them to return later in the day. When I heard that truck pulling back into town it made me happy, knowing that they would be home soon.

One year, my family had a wonderful Christmas while living in this house as we all got good gifts. I got a toy truck that I played with outside the house. I remember my older brother Jerry got a remote controlled car for his gift. He took it outside to try it out in the snow. The idea was probably to find out if it would operate like a real car. I went out there to see what the car would do in the snow.

He said, "Look at the tires spinning in the snow."

I replied, "Yeah, the car is sliding sideways and can't move forward."

He asked, "Do you want to try it out?"

I eagerly responded, "Yes" and tried it. I can still visualize the Christmas tree lights and the decorations my sisters and brother put up. I cannot forget the smell of food cooking, especially the yeast rolls and cookies.

Another thing about living there was getting ready to go over to the boarding school. We went there to watch the big Christmas program they put on for the community. There I got a bag containing peanuts, Christmas candy, an apple and an orange. My younger brothers Steve and Jake Jr. and I went with Mother while the older ones went with their friends. Another time during the Christmas holidays we all went to mother's employee's Christmas party. At this party I got a gift and a bag of goodies. One time during one of these parties my brother Jake Jr. was staying in the hospital. I was feeling happy to be there yet sad because he was not allowed to come home with us after the party.

Steve
and
Archie

I remember the third house my family lived in was a rock and cement-constructed building. There was a wooden porch with an overhang that provided shade on sunny days. I sat there in the shade with Mother and my brothers Steve and Jake Jr. waiting for Dad and the rest of the family to return.

Sometimes Dad and the older children worked on a lettuce and carrot farm out of town. One time I got a chance to go along for an overnight trip. I remember people were pulling carrots out of the ground and putting them into a crate. Somewhere near the farms they had a campground set up with a bunch of tents where people stayed overnight.

This house was located below the police station. Every now and then I saw a police car racing down the hill from the station. The police car would have its lights flashing and siren blaring away. We were also near the government's road department bullpen where the heavy equipment was parked at night or when not in use. In the same place there were different sizes of culverts lying around. My friends and I would always play among the culverts. We did this until we were told to get off by a man who was probably a security guard.

Living in that house, the smell of cooking fry bread was something else. We had it with pinto beans and the fry bread was always a treat. Today when I am cooking pork chops or hamburger meat in my mobile home the smell takes me back to my childhood. I would think about the times when Mom and Dad went to town on payday to shop. When they got home the older girls, Etta and Gracie, started preparing dinner. Yes, it would be pork chops or hamburger they were cooking. Sometimes they included fry bread, but not all the time.

During this time there were relatives visiting from Standing Rock, so the girls prepared a large meal. Dad almost always played his country music records on the phonograph. After dinner the older folks would sit around talking and visiting. Later on, probably when the drinks were brought out, they would start singing and dancing around.

The rest of us young ones went outside to play a game of softball. We boys, our cousins, and some friends together made two teams. We had a small field near the house where we played ball. One of my cousins, Henry, earned the nickname Heavy Hitter because each time it was his turn to bat he hit a home run. When it was his turn to bat we quickly moved back further into the outfield. We did this to try and catch the ball to put him out. One time, as we all backed up, he tricked us by hitting the ball just a short distance.

I recall one of the visits by our paternal grandparents, who came in their wagon and team of horses. They stayed with us for a few days and took care of personal business with Dad's help. One evening Grandpa Charles asked, "How come you don't know how to speak Navajo?"

I replied, "I don't know why," looking at him.

He said, "You boys need to start learning how to speak Navajo." When it was time to leave, I watched them connect the horses to the wagon. Getting aboard, they started back down the dirt road that led to Standing Rock about 20 miles away. The family piled into Dad's pickup truck later on to follow them. I always enjoyed sitting in the back of the truck near the tailgate, feeling the wind in my face. Dad caught up with Grandpa and asked, "Is it okay if the boys ride in the wagon with you?"

"Yes, that will be okay." We would be riding the wagon for about ten miles back to Grandpa's camp. I remember jumping off the wagon with my brothers and running alongside it. We would say, "Hey, we can run as fast as the wagon." Back then I had no idea that the horses had to pull at a certain pace to make it 20 miles.

I don't remember my maternal grandparents well. I would imagine that my older sisters and brother have stories about them. Sometimes, I used to ask Mother about my Grandfather Howard.

She would tell me that grandfather was a hard working man. Today, I can still visualize my paternal grandparents and certain relatives clearly. I am thinking this may be because I was closer to them than the rest of my relatives.

Living in that house, one of my cousins, Hazel, wanted me to take care of a little lamb. She explained, "All you have to do is fix it a bottle of milk everyday using powdered milk and water."

I replied, "Okay, but I have to ask Mom and Dad before anything else." Dad said it would be okay to keep the lamb.

I learned how to feed the little lamb using a pop bottle and a large nipple. I mixed the powdered milk and water carefully, then poured it into the pop bottle. After keeping up with this new chore the lamb knew when the milk was coming. With the help of my sister Etta the lamb had a bath on a regular basis. Back then this little lamb was probably the cleanest one for miles around. When I was old enough, I attended the summer recreations each summer. That summer, one of the scheduled events was a pet show..

I asked, "Dad, would it be okay to take the lamb to the summer recreation pet show?" He replied, "Yes it would be okay but don't let it run away."

I fastened a rope to the collar the lamb was wearing which had a small bell hanging on it. I looked at the lamb and said," Okay, little buddy, let's go and meet some other kids." The lamb looked at me as though if it understood what I said. By that time the lamb had gotten pretty used to me and others. I had no problem with the lamb when I took it to the pet show. In fact, the lamb won the second place prize. It was a red ribbon that had to be attached to my shirt. Some of the kids enjoyed the lamb while others thought it was stupid to bring it.

After the pet show I was on my way home with the lamb when a couple of girls, Cindy and Candy, stopped me. These girls were twin sisters and also Native American but not Navajo. The first twin, Cindy, asked, "Is it okay if we play with your lamb for a little while?" I did not say anything, but was looking at their bikes when a thought crossed my mind. I was thinking about switching off for a while because I wanted to ride their bikes.

I finally answered, "Okay, but one of you has to let me ride your bike." They looked at each other, at the lamb, then back at me. We stood there looking at each other, they on their bikes and me holding my lamb. Every now and then we heard the little bell which was hanging on the lamb's collar jingle.

Cindy finally said, "Okay you can ride my bike."

I happily replied, "Okay" and started to hand over the rope. Just then her sister, Candy, said, "You can ride mine, too." After all this, I took off riding around for a while then came back to them. Candy reminded me, "You can ride mine when you're ready." I replied, "Okay let's wait for a while."

Just then Candy asked, "Where did you get this cute little lamb?"

I replied, "My cousin gave it to me."

She added, "It sure is a clean little lamb."

"Yes, it is; my sister helps me bathe it."

She giggled and spoke again, "What kind of soap do you use?"

I answered, "I really don't know, I think it is some kind of Indian soap."

Her sister Candy asked, "What is your lamb's name?"

I replied, "We just call it little lamb in our own language."

She asked, "Do you know how to speak Navajo?"

I responded, "Not really, just a few words."

I rode the twin sisters' bikes around for a while, switching off from one bike to the other. It was about time for the three of us to be getting home. The girls both said, "Thank you for letting us play with your lamb."

I answered them, "Thank you for letting me ride your bikes! Maybe I will get one someday."

One of the twins replied, "I hope you get one – then we can all ride around together."

I agreed, saying, "Yeah, that would be fun." After messing around there for a while I took off with my lamb and headed home.

A few weeks later the little lamb was lying under my dad's truck when my sister Etta drove off. The lamb did not get out in time so it got run over. It got pretty banged up and died quickly. I remember crying for my little buddy. I did not realize that a person can get pretty attached to an animal. My relatives promised me another lamb during the next lambing season.

One thing the family had that I was proud of was a black and white television set. The family would watch it together, especially on Friday or Saturday nights. I remember there would be a western movie with cowboys and Indians. Sometimes, after school, the boys and I watched *The Little Rascals*, a favorite of many. The boys would choose one of the characters and pretend to be him.

When our relatives from Standing Rock would visit, the kids got a chance to watch cartoons on Saturday morning. My cousin Rose would say, "I like to come with my mom and dad so I can watch television."

I replied, "It is okay to have a television but we don't watch it all the time." I recall one of the older family members standing outside turning the antenna to get the clearest picture.

Someone else would be inside watching the television to let them know when this occurred. Dad had several tricks to try and keep all us kids happy despite the living conditions. I think Mother was at work most of the time.

I also recall that when Thursday afternoon came around some of us boys would run to the community house before other boys got there. We did this to set up chairs for the movie they showed every Thursday night. If we made it there on time to set up the chairs, this meant a free movie pass, a bag of popcorn and a bottle of soda pop. After every one left the community house we helped clean up. The community house served many people on different occasions. It was a good place to hang out; sometimes teenagers listened to the jukebox and danced. Back then it cost a quarter to play three songs. Sometimes with a couple of friends we challenged ourselves by taking on a large puzzle. I remember some of these puzzles had small pieces. There were several table games made available for the community to use. One day Leonard, who worked there, stated, "If you boys take care of all these things then they will be here for the next person to enjoy."

When I was around the age of 11 or 12 we moved to the fourth and probably the best house we lived in while I was growing up. It had a large living room, four bedrooms, bathroom and a kitchen area. I shared a bedroom with my brother Steve. We had a bunk bed set up in our room and one time I fell off the top bunk in my sleep.

The house sat above the ground several feet so there were porches with steps in the front and back.

In the front yard there were two large trees that I climbed with my brothers Steve and Jake Jr. During the nighttime with a couple of friends, we would sit in one of those trees watching people go by. Other times Dad would let us boys with a couple of friends set up a tent in the front yard. One time we were sitting in the tent at night when a policeman approached us. He asked, "What are you boys doing out here late at night?"

I replied, "My Dad knows we are out here."

Doubtful, he inquired, "Are you sure?"

I courageously answered, "Yes, sir, I am not lying to you." Without saying anything else he just drove off down the road. I recall this incident because we were listening to rock and roll music on my friend's Ron's transistor radio.

Around this time, there was something in the air about our country, Russia and Cuba. I really did not understand what was going on between the countries. Some of my friends were saying, "My dad might have to go back to the army for a while." Later on I found out that it was the missile crises between the United States and Russia. I guess at the last minute everything sort of canceled out.

While living in that house I invited my friends John and Andrew over to play or watch some television. Sometimes with my friends John and Donald we had a miniature basketball tournament in my bedroom. We used a small ball and a small homemade backboard and goal. The backboard was made from a hard cardboard. The goal was usually made from a clothes hanger. One of the boys actually knitted the net to the goal. We drew a tournament bracket then drew numbers to see where we would be placed. We got pretty good in getting the small ball through the small goal from a fair distance. Unknowingly this would improve our shots when we played on a regular size basketball court.

While we lived in that house the community received information about starting a Boy Scout troop. I was old enough so I asked Dad if it would be okay to join. I joined with some friends and my brother Jerry; we got a

Scoutmaster and some volunteers to help the troop. One of the first things we did was have a Scout meeting. After introductions the meeting turned toward a discussion about how we could raise some funds. They were needed to purchase the Scouting equipment we lacked. Some of us could not afford to buy scouting equipment. The Scoutmaster, Mr. Albert, volunteers, Scouts and family members pulled together to organize a fundraising event. The best fundraising event the whole group did was an enchilada plate sale. This special event brought in a good amount of money. I think the majority of the community enjoyed the enchilada dinner. I think this was the first time I tasted homemade enchiladas.

The purpose of the fundraising was to make sure each Scout was well-equipped for hiking expedition or an overnight camping trip. Plans were made to purchase enough camping equipment to meet any demand. We needed equipment like sleeping bags, backpacks, cooking utensils, small shovels, axes, first aid kits and others. After making enough money from our fundraising events and contributions from the community, we were ready to go shopping. To purchase the equipment we all went to the US Army surplus store in Gallup. There they had everything we needed plus more.

Most of the Scouts were able to have their parents purchase a Scout uniform with identification patches and a handbook. The uniform was worn with a neckerchief wrapped around the shoulders and a knot tied in the front.

At this point the troop did not have a specific neckerchief. Later during a regular Scout meeting the choice was to wear a bright turquoise one.

I still recall how the green scout uniform and the turquoise colored neckerchief matched so well. Lillian, the spouse of one of the volunteers, made and donated the neckerchiefs to the troop. One of the Scouts brought a bunch of round-shaped cow bones to use with the neckerchief. The Scouts dressed up the bones using different approaches like painting, carving and bead work. The newly designed bones were used instead of a square knot to keep the neckerchief in place.

The Scouts were randomly divided into different groups. I became a member of the Lion patrol with a couple of close buddies, Ted and Rob. Each patrol chose a patrol leader and made a patrol flag. At each Scout meeting or outing, the patrol flag had to be visible. I remember we all had to start off as tenderfeet. It was up to us individually to move upward on the rank scale.

All the Scouts with their patrols were ready and well-equipped to go out on their first camping trip. All packed and ready, off I went with my patrol and the rest of the Scouts to Blue Water Lake. We found a place away from the regular camping and picnic grounds back in the wooded area near the lake. Upon arrival I helped pitch tents and gather fire wood. With all the tents pitched and camp fires illuminating the night we were ready to prepare our meals for the evening. We were allowed to help our fellow Scouts only if they were having real problems. Whatever it was we prepared, it was going to be checked by our Scoutmaster, Mr. Albert. Here I got a chance to use one of the new cooking utensils the Scouts purchased.

I cooked some hamburger meat and added some potatoes and corn for my meal. Camp fires burning in the night in front of each tent looked and felt so good. It was nearly time to turn in for the night so I double checked my stuff before I did.

Bright and early the next morning the Scoutmaster shouted out, "Rise and shine, troop, we need to get started for a hiking adventure." I heard that so I pulled myself out of my sleeping bag and quickly got myself ready. I was checking my food supplies to cook myself some breakfast. Just then the Scoutmaster informed us, "You guys can pick up something to cook for breakfast over here."

Getting out of my tent I asked, "What do you have, sir?"

He replied, "Some raw bacon, sausage and eggs."

One of the volunteers, Mr. McDonal, said, "I have some biscuits and potatoes over here, so come get some." I grabbed some of the goodies to prepare my meal.

A fellow Scout, Bruce, cheerfully said, "I brought some juice that my mother told me to share with the gang."

I said, "Boy this is fun to cook a meal outdoors with the other Scouts."

Everything put in place with the tent fastened up tightly, I grabbed my backpack, saying enthusiastically, "I am ready to go on that hiking expedition."

A couple of the volunteers stayed back to keep an eye on our campsite. Turning towards them I teasingly said, "Hey, I bet you guys are probably going fishing huh?"

One of them answered, "You got that right."

I jokingly replied, "Catch a bunch of fish – maybe it will be good for a fish cookout this evening."

They both laughed and said, "We will try." Afterwards I thought to myself, *why did I say that?* because I didn't even know how fish cooked like that tasted. From camp we started upstream to hike back into the canyon between the mountains somewhere south of camp.

Walking along the stream, I said, "Hey, you guys, look in the water and you can see the fish right there."

Another Scout, James, stated, "It would be good to catch a few of these fish to add to our evening meal."

I replied, "Yeah, but I really don't know how to cook fish."

He responded, "You don't know how to cook fish, huh? Man, it is the best."

I said, "I have not really gone fishing anywhere."

He said, "If I catch some I will show you how to clean and cook it."

"Okay, I guess I can try and learn," I replied, thinking to myself no way, buddy.

I was out there most of the day finding out different things about nature. I saw different kinds and sizes of animal tracks and plants. I saw where lightning had struck a tree some time ago, splitting it right down the middle. I said, "Hey guys, I was told not to touch or bother trees that were struck by lightning."

One of the Scouts, Arthur asked, "Why is that?"

I replied, "It has something to do with getting sick from it after touching it." I still recall my parents told us kids one time on a family picnic outing about lightning. Back then I remember Dad firmly stated, "You're not supposed to bother or use any part of a tree that was struck by lightning." The sky was clear and blue so I did not worry about rain or lightning.

Arriving back at camp I started getting situated for the night. I prepared myself a small meal of hot dogs and beans. The volunteers who stayed back caught several fish as did some of the Scouts. That brought on a good fish fry with plenty to go around. I did not like the smell of the fish so I did not eat any. My friend Ted said, "Hey, dude, you are really missing out."

I replied, "Missing out, huh?"

He repeated, "Yes, sir, missing out big time."

I stated, "I really don't want to try any right now; maybe next time."

When it got dark enough the Scoutmaster and the volunteers, using flashlights, introduced to us what I think was Morse code. Each patrol got a chance to try sending and receiving messages. I remember I tried signaling with some difficulty and I thought to myself that it would take hours of practice.

We used a guidebook filled with dots and dashes to send and receive messages. It was difficult but fun trying to figure out the messages. After it was all over I remember shining the flash light across part of the lake. The light displayed a weird picture of the little waves rippling.

To me this felt sort of scary, staying near the lake at night. This may have been because the lake was a large one. I did not mention that to anyone as I thought they might call me a sissy if I did. It did not bother me to be near the lake during the daytime.

There were several more adventure camping trips my older brother Jerry and I went on with the Scouts. I remember the Mount Taylor trip because snow was in the forecast. Some of the parents back in Crownpoint were feeling a little uncomfortable about the weather. We arrived at our campsite early Friday evening and there was hardly any snow except on the peak. We pitched up our tents and gathered firewood. We got our campfires going so we could cook our meals. I shared a tent with a good friend of mine, Ted. He asked, "What are you going to cook?"

I replied, "Probably some potatoes and something to go with it."

He said, "I brought a bunch of hamburger meat."

I replied, "Is that right? It sure sounds good!"

He generously said, "Yeah, you are welcome to cook some."

"Great I'll cook some hamburgers and potatoes to eat."

He responded, "That sounds good; I'll help you cook."

"Okay, then let's get started; I am hungry."

He asked, "What about bread?"

I replied, "I brought some, and if we need more, I think the Scoutmaster brought extra." We cooked hamburgers, potatoes and warmed up a can of beans. We also got some yellow chili peppers from my older brother to complete our meal.

It was nice to see a bunch of campfires burning in the night at the same time. My older brother told my buddy and me to get extra firewood. I packed some of this firewood in our tent to keep it dry. I was glad I took the time to do that because it paid off the next morning. We had some snowfall over night that covered everything around camp.

We were able to get our campfire going before some

of the other Scouts. After we got a nice fire going, I said to my friend Ted, "What shall we cook for breakfast?"

He asked, "What else do you have with you?"

I told him, "A can of lunch meat, some eggs, some potatoes and water."

He responded, "Good, I have some juice, biscuits and gravy mix."

I said, "I guess we can put some of this food together." We ended up frying some potatoes, mixing in some lunch meat and eggs. He added some juice, biscuits and gravy. Feeling content I stated, "You know what this might be better than eating at some café, huh?"

He laughed and said, "Yeah, it might be." After eating, we quickly cleaned up our mess and put our things away.

After we got our gear squared away and placed back in the tent, I turned to our neighbors and said, "Hey, guys, do you hear those wild turkeys out there somewhere?"

One of them replied, "I can see them right over there in that large tree," and pointed in that direction. I looked toward where he was pointing and said, "Wow, you are right!" They appeared not to be afraid of us but some of them took off and disappeared into the woods. There were some deer tracks near our camp in the light snow that fell overnight. The snow was not really an issue at this point as most of us were used to it. Growing up in Crownpoint we usually got a good amount of snow during the winter time.

It was Saturday so the Scouts went on a hiking expedition in the woods. Here we found out more about animal tracks and plants that lived on this peak.

There were deer, turkey, rabbit and other small animal tracks and more snow as we hiked higher. To avoid any problems we might encounter, we did not go too far up. I can still see the brightness coming off the snow during the day and extra darkness of the night. I think the Scouts all had lunch meat sandwiches to eat for a quick lunch provided by the Scoutmaster.

We all started back toward camp later in the day. We wanted to be back before it got too dark so we could get our campfires going. When we got close to camp I told my partner, Ted, we should pick up some firewood.

He said, "You are right; that's a good idea." We asked the Scoutmaster if we could do that.

He stated, "That is a good idea and the others should do the same."

One of the scouts Ray asked, "Do what?"

The Scoutmaster replied, "Start picking up some firewood." My partner and I picked up a good amount and tied it together in a bundle. We took turns dragging the firewood back to camp. We all got back to camp and started getting our campfires going.

My partner and I cooked the rest of the hamburger meat so it would not go to waste. My partner asked, "How was the hamburger?"

I replied, "It tastes good, especially cooking it out here over a campfire."

He said, "My mother told me to get some meat from the store for my trip so I got a bunch of hamburger meat."

I said, "Be sure to thank your mom for the hamburger meat."

He responded, "Yes, I will" and laughed. That night

the scouts did not do too much and it seemed like we were all tired.

Sitting around the campfire, every now and then someone would say, "Hey, does anyone want some of this to eat?" As the night went on the Scouts slowly started disappearing into their tents until everybody went off to sleep.

Sunday morning the Scoutmaster informed us, "It will not be necessary to build anymore camp fires; we can use mine." One of the volunteers, Mr. Smith, must have gotten up extra early to he prepare some biscuit sandwiches stuffed with bacon and eggs. He shouted out, "Okay, boys, come and get it before it's all gone." After eating our fill we all told him, "Good job on the biscuit sandwiches."

He replied, "I think this might be your lucky day – you won't have to do any more cooking." Just then the Scoutmaster, Mr. Albert, informed us, "I have a surprise set up for you guys."

James asked curiously, "What do you mean by 'surprise'?"

Mr. Albert replied, "I will tell you all about it when we get there." We were all in agreement, and made sure our camp fires were completely out.

We took down our tents and packed our things in his truck. With everything packed securely we started down the road. It seem like we drove for several miles then out of nowhere some log cabins appeared. He said, "Here we are boys," and shut off his truck. There were some people here and it appeared that they were pretty busy doing something. The Scoutmaster said, "These people are my relatives and they live here."

One of the scouts asked, "Are you saying we were camping on your land?"

He responded, "Yes, something like that." After that camping adventure I thought to myself, these people have some pretty land.

The Scoutmaster talked with these people for a while then returned saying "Hey, you guys, follow me over to that cabin." We all followed him and went in and sat down at some tables that were set up. Much to our surprise, his relatives were going to feed all of us. There were all different kinds of food to eat which tasted very good. Afterwards we all thanked the people for their hospitality. One of them said, "You guys are welcome to come back to visit." With our tummies full we made it back to the trucks we were riding in. The Scoutmaster talked with these people awhile, then told them, "We need to be getting back."

We were on the road for several hours making our way home. Most of the guys fell a sleep on the way home which may be because of all the good food we ate. On the way home the snow got deeper as we approached Satan's canyon.

When my older brother and I got home our parents said, "Everybody was talking about the snow and your camping trip."

I asked, "Were you guys worried about us being out there?"

Dad confidently responded, "We were, but not that much because of the people you were with." The good thing about this trip was that some of the volunteers worked for the government roads department.

Another memorable camping trip I went on with

the Scouts was in the Chuska Mountains, a mountain range located along the New Mexico and Arizona border. We camped out there for a whole week at a special camp site. Scouts came from the surrounding area and from across the Navajo reservation. I can still see tents pitched up everywhere with campfire smoke rising into the sky. This special camping event took place during the summer months so it was beautiful up there.

There were different events planned for the week to challenge our Scouting skills. The Scouts were there to try and win some of these events individually or as teams.

One morning after breakfast we all met at the main point of the campsite. We were given special instructions about going on a survival hike and overnight camping exercise. There were several Scoutmasters who searched our backpacks. We were only allowed to take certain items on this adventure. I remember some of us Scouts had junk food like chips, soda pop and candy bars. All these items were taken away from us before we left. We hiked most of the day and had a quick lunch somewhere along the trail. When we arrived at an unfamiliar place in the wilderness we joined back up with our troop. The Scouts pitched up their tents everywhere; that looked pretty neat.

We were given only one match to start our campfires. We were also given some raw meat, potatoes, and aluminum foil to prepare a meal. A fellow Scout, Bruce, and I put our match and food together. This way we were able to start our camp fire and cook our meal. At first it was kind of difficult to get started but we managed. The next morning we were given some more raw food and aluminum foil. We did the same thing by putting the food together and then cooking it. After breakfast all the Scouts took down their tents and packed everything.

We were divided into different groups and were given maps to follow back to the main camp site. My group got together to discuss the map before we left. That way we would know what to do during our journey back so we could move along quickly. At one point we had some difficulty trying to locate a mark that was supposed to be on a large tree or rock.

Finally the mark was located at the bottom of a large tree, hidden by some leaves. A Scout, Larry, shouted out, "Here it is under, these leaves."

Another scout, Tommy, asked, "How did you find it right there?"

Larry replied, "I noticed there were green leaves among dead ones and this did not look right."

The rest of us agreed stating, "Good job; now you can be the leader." After that incident we were able to make it the rest of the way rather smoothly. Overall the exercise turned out to be interesting.

Our troop entered the human pyramid building contest earlier in the week. All week long we were challenged by various troops and we beat most of them. The troop was able to make it to the finals. I was the one who had to climb to the top of the pyramid. On the final night of competition we were up against another troop to determine the champs.

The whistle blew for us to start building. Each scout quickly jumped into position on the pyramid. All set I made my climb upward and made it to the top. When I reached the top I threw my arms up to signal completion. At that very second I lost my balance; I slipped and fell to the ground. I just laid there on the ground where I hit, catching my breath.

One of the Scoutmasters came over and asked, "Are you all right? I think you hit pretty hard."

I laid there and replied, "I'll be all right in a little bit." Just then, my friend, Ted, interrupted, "Aw, come on, buddy, you can tough it out."

Embarrassed, I responded, "Yeah," and started to get up. Because of that no human building pyramid champ was declared. Determined to win, the troop eagerly stated, "Let's try it again." We were given another chance and that time I did not slip; we easily beat the scouts.

Before long the family left Crownpoint. We moved out of the government quarters and moved to Standing Rock where we had relatives. There at the camp we did not have a home of our own to live in. A place to stay had to be a relative's Hogan or small house. Whatever it had to be, that was going to be home for us. I can recall those structures were pretty small. Today some of the houses are still there but the majority of the families have relocated. Most of them left to find employment away from the reservation because of the limited job opportunities back home.

Chapter Three
School And Summer Days

The Crownpoint Elementary School provided education to students from kindergarten to the ninth grade. I had my first taste of school during the fall of 1956, as I turned five earlier that year and became old enough to start school. So, I was enrolled at the Crownpoint Elementary School in the kindergarten class. Most of the teachers were non-Native Americans. Before school started I was away from home most of the time when I played with friends. When I started school I did not like it at all. Eventually, somehow, I was able to get used to that new routine. I slowly got to know some of the new students and teachers.

At the beginning of the school year I was measured for a complete set of clothes provided by the Navajo Tribe Clothing Program. After several weeks went by the teacher, Mrs. Penny, called out names of certain students and I was included. I got my set of clothes, a pair of shoes, a coat, and a pair of rubber boots for the snow. I don't remember how I got my clothes home but I think the teacher packed them in a plastic bag. After attending school for a while I learned that the first thing to do when I got home was change out of my school clothes into play clothes.

One day I arrived at school looking pretty rugged, wearing dirty clothes, so the teacher, Mrs. Penny, pulled me aside. She whispered, "Let's go and see Mary, the school nurse." I ended up taking a bath there.

After taking my bath the nurse gave me a complete set of new clothes and I went back to my classroom. After school I went home and took my old clothes with me. Mother asked, "What happened and where did you get the new clothes?" I told her everything that took place that day and gave her a note from the teacher.

I was happy with the new clothes especially the shirt as it was a dark blue one. I think what happened that morning was that I did not bother to change back into my school clothes. I probably did not get cleaned up from the day before or I was just being a kid.

During my first few years of school, I made several new friends with both the boys and girls who caught the school bus as we played during recess time.. Often the students teased each other about being someone's boyfriend or girlfriend. Some of the students would call me little Archie, like the kid in the comic books. One of them would always say, "Where is your girlfriend Veronica or Betty?" Sometimes I would get mad and other times, I just did not listen to them.

The playground was something else as we played on the monkey bars, the swings, the slide and chased each other around. We also enjoyed messing around on the teeter-totter and the merry-go-round. I enjoyed having recess time twice a day and some playtime after lunch. When I did not do my school work or called other students names, I had to stay inside and clean the chalk-boards with whoever else was being punished. After being punished, one of the girls, Vicky, always reminded us guys that we were stupid for getting into trouble.

Christmas was always a big thing as I participated in the annual Christmas play according to grade level. The Christmas play was presented by the school for the community. During this time, I dressed up as one of the little elves and sat in the class group and helped with singing. When I advanced in grade level, I got a chance to be one of the shepherds. I dressed up like a real shepherd just like the ones I saw in the picures on Christmas cards. The teachers at this school had some good talent as they got us ready for the play. At different times, I was part of the choir, singing Christmas carols with the rest of the students and teachers. For some reason, after it was all over I felt a sense of loneliness.

Another special event during the Christmas season was getting a chance to travel to Gallup High School to sing in a Christmas choir. The choir consisted of sixth graders from different schools in the county. That Christmas play was probably one of the largest plays I would see at that time. After the play I got back on the school bus with a sack lunch to eat, prepared by the school. The bus ride back to Crownpoint was fun and maybe because I sat with one of the girls, Mickey. We talked and laughed most of the time on the way home. As usual the other students started teasing us about being girlfriend and boyfriend. I liked being friends with the students but if they treated me mean, then I treated them the same way.

At the end of the school year, another special event was having a field day full of different outdoor activities. There I competed in different field events according to grade level. Some events included running races, high jumping, tossing a baseball, three-legged races, a gunny-sack race, tug-of-war and so forth. Some students won ribbons or other prizes.

During these events the school cooks would prepare hamburgers and hot dogs outside which made it seem like a giant picnic. Some parents volunteered to help with the activities or with the cooking. After eating hamburgers, hot dogs, watermelon and punch, the students sat around in the upper grade level playground watching different events. Eventually, I participated in more events as I grew older. I won a ribbon or two in individual events like races or in team efforts like tug-of-war. The field day, as it was called back then, was an annual event at the good old Crownpoint Elementary School and meant school was out for the summer.

Attending Crownpoint Elementary was not all fun and games. There was a part where I had to learn how to do different schoolwork. I remember I started by learning the alphabet and to count numbers orally. It was always a competition between the girls and boys. I think the girls were more serious about school than some of us boys. Trying to do some of the alphabet or counting orally was hard because there was always a class joker making us laugh. Eventually, I learned the two and went on to writing my name, address, and parents' names.

In one of the earlier grade levels there was a spelling book with different words in it for me to learn. I think I liked this book because of the color and the clear writing it contained. I was quizzed on the words each Friday morning with the rest of the class. Being quizzed and allowing myself practice time, I got pretty good at spelling. Next was to learn how to add and subtract numbers using flash cards or writing them on the chalk board.

I enjoyed competing against the girls at the chalk board. Somewhere along the line I learned how to read as the rest of the students and I did oral reading. Eventually as I progressed upward in grade level I learned more and more about arithmetic, spelling, writing and reading.

In one of my classes we had to write a letter to someone who lived away from Crownpoint. I decided to write a letter to my paternal grandpa, Charles, who lived in Standing Rock. I did not know how to spell his first name so I asked one of the students with the same first name to help me. I completed the letter, addressed the envelope and mailed it off. I never heard if my grandpa got the letter and I never asked him if he did when I saw him.

The students were also encouraged to participate in school activities, including school plays, choirs, sports, science fairs and artwork. I volunteered and participated in different classroom plays. One play I remember was when we did *Hansel and Gretel* and I got a chance to be Hansel. In one scene the old witch dragged me out of the gingerbread house to lock me up in a little shed. The audience responded by clapping when they saw her dragging me by my feet. I was trying to get away from her but she had a good hold on my ankles. She demanded, "Come on you little brat," and jerked my ankles a little. The audience enjoyed the plays that consisted of students and parents. During the play, the house in which the old witch lived was covered with real gingerbread men and candy. At the end of the performance I got a nice gingerbread man from the teacher.

I took the gingerbread man home as I wanted to share it with Dad when he came home from work. I tried saving it but in time I gave in and shared it with Mickey.

While attending that school I played basketball and ran track on the sixth and seventh grade teams. I enjoyed competing against the different schools in the local school district. During practice I worked hard for both sports so I could remain on the team. I always enjoyed the home games which gave all the players a chance to play.

One beautiful spring day, not expecting anything, I was doing class activities with other students when I was told to get on the Standing Rock bus after school. I found out later that my family had moved back to Standing Rock where I had relatives. Standing Rock is located on the reservation about 20 miles west of Crownpoint. When class let out I caught the school bus back to Standing Rock and got off at the trading post.

I started walking with my brother Jerry down the dirt road that led to our relatives' camp. The walk was long and hot and when we finally arrived no one was around. Our family's belonging were stacked up next to a relative's house. I sat against the family's belongings with my older brother, wondering what had happened. The stuff was unevenly stacked and it appeared like someone was in a rush to unload. Eventually, I got tired and fell asleep somewhere among our belongings. Until the rest of the family came back later in the day I had no idea where we were going to live.

Standing Rock, Standing Rock, NM

It seemed that the relatives who lived there did not have any kind of utilities. They used a kerosene lamp for lighting their homes at night. They used firewood to do their cooking. They had to haul drinking water from somewhere. Where they kept their food, like meat, I had no idea.

I became confused because of the sudden changes. I think we stayed in a hogan or somewhere but I know it was pretty small. Being there, the first thing I noticed was the quietness and the smell of the sheep corral that I did not like. Steve, Jake Jr. and I did not know how to speak the Navajo language and this kind of complicated our communication with relatives.

For the next two months, my three brothers and sister Gracie and I had to finish out the school year from there. We had no choice but to catch the school bus from Standing Rock to Crownpoint. We lived about three miles from the Standing Rock Trading Post where the school bus stopped to pick up the students. This meant we had to get up early and get to the bus stop in time to catch the bus. I think there was no vehicle to drive us to the bus stop each day so we walked. I often walked and ran to the bus stop alone to catch the bus. Sometimes my younger brothers stayed back because it was hard on them. Sometimes I took a shortcut and had to pass by some cows or horses. They would look at me as though they wanted to run over me. This made me feel sort of scared so I looked straight ahead. My sister Gracie and brother Jerry often stayed with friends in Crownpoint.

I managed to make it to school every day in spite of what happened and had perfect attendance for the school year. Each student in my sixth grade class got a Payday candy bar at the end of the school year. The teacher, Mr. Sage, gave me an extra one for having perfect attendance. When the school bell rang I stood up from my desk to leave the classroom. I slowly made my way toward the school bus to go back to Standing Rock. I really did not want to go back there but had no choice.

For the time being we had to live in a small house. I missed the last house we lived in at Crownpoint, as it was a nice house. The small place at Standing Rock had no utilities whatsoever. As I got closer to the bus, I felt lonely because I never had to catch a bus to go home at the end of the school year. I did not really know what happened that caused the family to move. I was curious, wanting to ask my parents but changed my mind.

During the first summer at Standing Rock, my younger brothers and I would go along with our cousins Marie and Ronnie when they herded the sheep to the watering hole. The watering hole was located about four miles north of camp. When we got there I noticed other kids had their families' flocks there also. The other kids would say something to us, speaking the Navajo language, which none of us boys understood. Marie did her best to interpret what was being said. I was curious about the water so I found a tin can to taste it even after I had been warned. I did not know why the sheep liked to drink that water because it was very salty. My younger brothers and I tagged along with my cousins when they took the sheep out for grazing, probably because there was nothing to do back at camp.

Sometimes we all went with Grandma Bess when she took the sheep for dipping. The sheep dipping was some form of vaccination that the government used at that time. There were several families with their herd of sheep waiting to get their sheep vaccinated. Some of the families would butcher one of their sheep.

There would be enough to prepare a large meal to feed the helpers and whoever wanted to eat some mutton. The meals prepared were roast mutton and mutton stew which at the time had an unusual odor. One time we talked our cousins into letting us ride the sheep before they got to the watering hole. That was fun but the bad thing about it was how we smelled afterward.

Summer concluded and it was time to go back to school. I was placed at Manuelito Hall with my older brother when school started again. Manuelito Hall was a government dormitory located in Gallup. I cried often as I did not like being away from the rest of the family. Many Navajo Native American boys and girls were housed at Manuelito Hall so they could attend the Gallup Public Schools. The dormitory was a two-story building shaped like the capital letter H. One side was the girl's dorm with the younger girls living on the lower floor. Likewise the boy's side had the younger boys living on the lower floor. Altogether it held at least 500 students ranging from kindergarten to the twelfth grade. Each student had a bunk bed and locker that were set along the outer wall with an aisle running down the middle.

Later I found out that Manuelito Hall was one of many border town dormitories that were situated in New Mexico, Arizona, and Colorado. These government dormitories provided room and board for any Native American student who wanted to attend school.

I slowly got used to being away from the family and began to like the dormitory lifestyle. I got a chance to take a daily shower, do laundry, eat three meals a day and had my own bed. Being there made sense compared to walking a long distance to catch the school bus. Each student staying at the dormitory had a daily chore to do somewhere on campus. The chores had to be completed before catching the school bus.

On Saturday mornings, it was the major clean up day followed by an inspection. We got up extra early to grab a mop, broom and bucket, or else we would have to wait for one. After passing the inspection the weekend was ours to do homework, laundry or go on school activities. Most of the students were involved in some form of activity. Those who did not pass inspection were sort of grounded for the rest of the weekend and had to remain at the dorm.

When I came to Manuelito Hall I only spoke the English language and very few words of Navajo, but soon started learning how to speak Navajo with help from other students. Sometimes one of the boys would tell me how to say something in Navajo and usually it was incorrect or something bad. The dorm girls helped by letting me know that I was saying something bad so they corrected me. After stumbling a few more times I quit listening to the boys. Instead I asked some of the girls who had become my friends. They showed their interest in helping me with our native language.

Eventually I made more friends with the dorm students. Somewhere along the line I found out that some of the students that attended Crownpoint boarding school were also staying there. I started to hang around with the girls and boys who came from the Crownpoint area. As time went on I got used to staying there, probably because of making more friends. Some of the girls or boys would buy me a soda pop and a bag of chips from the canteen. The first time I heard one of the students use the word canteen I thought of water. I did not go home on weekends or when there was short break from school like others students did.

I started my seventh grade year at Central Junior High where only seventh graders attended. My first day there was very different from my old school. Instead of being in the same classroom with the same teacher the entire day, I had to change classrooms for each course taken and had a different teacher for each class. The majority of the students were non-Native Americans. I was probably experiencing some anxiety and intimidation. I did not like being here but I had no choice. I often told my friends how I felt. They would tell me in that time I would get used to it. Another student, Albert, shared that, "I felt the same way the first time I came to stay at the dorm." However, as time went on I made friends with some of the non-Native Americans students.

While attending this school I wanted to be a Wildcat so I tried out for the basketball team. Tryouts went on for a whole week and at the end of each session I waited to be chosen. Again and again I failed to make the team, but I kept trying up to the last day, putting out my best. On the last day the coach, Mr. Watson, informed me, "You are a good player but my roster is full." I felt bad because I thought I was not good enough to become a Wildcat.

I told one of the dorm attendants, Mr. Lewis, about my experience with the basketball tryouts at school. He said, "In case you did not know, I coach the girls' and boys' junior high basketball team for the dorm."

"Is that right? That's great!" I replied.

He added, "If you would like to be a Trojan instead of a Wildcat, come out to the gym tonight and sign up."

I said, "I will be there; what do I have to bring?"

"You don't have to bring anything. I'll have everything there."

"Thanks. I'll see you at the gym." Later in the evening I went to the gym to sign up for the team. Everyone who signed up attended practice right after school every day for two weeks.

Eventually I made the team to play ball for the dorm. Some of the other students who did not make the school team also got a chance to play ball there. These guys were pretty good ballplayers so I was wondering why they did not make the school team. I felt that these guys could help me to be a better player myself.

The dormitory had both girls' and boys' junior and senior high basketball teams. Being on the team, I got a chance to travel to the different dormitories to play against them on the weekends. After making the team and playing with these guys, I did not feel left out after all. The Trojan girls' and boys' teams traveled together in one bus with one coach. Both teams played in many tournaments during the season. This gave me a chance to visit different parts of the Navajo reservation in Arizona. We boys played well together, as well as the girls, so we won many of our games. When we played at the Albuquerque dorm my cousin Anita was there. At the time she was attending one of the Albuquerque schools so she stayed at their dorm. She was all excited when she saw me so she started cheering for our team. We were down by a couple of points with only a few minutes left to play. By scoring some quick baskets we managed to win the game. Afterward, my cousin came up to me and cheerfully stated, "It sure is nice to see you!"

One special annual event which took place at the dorm was the all-border-town-dormitories' high school girls' and boy's basketball tournament. My brother Jerry got a chance to play for the Vikings before he finished school. During the tournament the weekend was full of activities throughout the campus.

Basketball players came from different dormitories and many from different Indian tribes. The basketball tournament went on for three days, followed by a dance. There everyone enjoyed dancing and having refreshments. I can still taste the cake and punch served to everyone.

My parents had gone through a divorce during the first year we were all attending school away from home. Mother moved away to work at one of the government schools somewhere north of Crownpoint.

She lived in the government quarters at the school where she was working. When we boys got a chance we stayed with her for a few days. I spent more time at Standing Rock to help Dad and Grandma haul drinking water, chop firewood and do other chores. By that time I think I was starting to adjust to this type of living.

When my seventh grade year concluded Dad, my older sister Etta, my younger brother Steve and I traveled somewhere into Utah. We all went there to work on a strawberry and cherry farm for the summer. Dad had an old truck but he kept it in fair running condition. In this truck the family packed some belongings and went to Gallup. We all got to Gallup and found a place to camp out after Dad got some information. He had to find out where we were supposed to meet some people the next morning. The next morning we met some people from Utah, who were going to take us back with them to work. Gracie and Jerry took the truck home with them.

Dad let them use it for their summer employment at the chapter house.

On our way to Utah we rode in back of a pickup truck with a camper on it. We stopped along the way to stretch our legs and grab a sandwich. We finally got to our destination in the early evening. There were three pickup trucks following each other all the way from Gallup. Each pickup truck contained a different family from the Gallup area. Upon arriving in Utah, we were all situated in a large house that was sectioned off so we had our own private entrance.

The families who lived in the same area with us looked after one another. As time went on, my younger brother and I got to know the other kids well. One family that worked there consisted of the mother, two older daughters and three younger boys. I made some extra money for myself by giving her boys haircuts, something I had learned to do while living in the dorm.

My younger brother and I helped as much as we could and sometimes we just messed around with the other kids there. My brother and I managed to pick enough strawberries to fill several crates and did the same when we picked cherries. We were told if we worked hard this would mean a new pair of cowboy boots for school. The strawberry fields and cherry orchards had different kinds of people picking. Some of the workers said they were either high school or college students. I made friends with some of the girls and boys over time. It was not always work because we had our strawberry and cherry fights among us boys and girls. Someone with a handful of strawberries would sneak up on someone and rub the berries in their face. This went on until we were all covered with crushed strawberries. Sometimes early in the morning my brother and I would take off into the cherry orchard. There we would climb a tree and eat cherries until we'd had enough.

I recall an irrigation canal that ran near the house where we lived. My younger brother and I, with some of the other kids, would go swimming in the cold water that ran in the canal. The water was cold at first but it felt good after a while because the weather was hot. We got to mess around along the canal several more times until a man told us to stay out of the canal. He firmly stated, "The water is dangerous, especially at the bottom where the current is swift." Then he added, "Down the way a bit the water runs into a hole in the ground." He suggested that we should try the city pool where there would be a lifeguard on duty. We guys took the man's advice and went over to the city swimming pool. It was a very large swimming pool with a lot of people of different ages. They were swimming or just lying around in the sun. We were having fun until some of the local kids started picking on us and calling us names. We did not like what we were being called so we got into a fight with some of them. When a couple of the local kids started to cry, they all ran away from us. After this ordeal they never picked on us again.

When a carnival came into town so Dad took us boys there to enjoy some of the rides. Along with our friends, my younger brother and I disappeared into the crowd to check out the rides. While at the carnival, Dad ran into some people we worked with so they went for a drive somewhere. After a few hours passed we all got back together and went back to where we stayed. I think each of us guys won a prize or two and had some goodies to eat. This carnival was different from the ones back home because there were very few Native Americans.

I enjoyed being there because it was fun and something different to do. At the end of the summer it was time to leave Utah and return to our home in Standing Rock.

I guess we made enough money for dad to buy a used car. I remember it was a turquoise and white Chevrolet two-door coupe. We left Utah and drove most of the night. Early the next morning we got close to where mother lived near the Four Corners area. Unfortunately the car gave out on us so Dad flagged down a passing car. He asked the occupants if they could deliver a message to Mother. The people in the car helpfully stated, "We will be more then glad to do that for you." Dad gave them the phone number where to contact Mother. We stayed beside the road until Mother came in her pickup truck. They connected a towing chain to the car and pulled it about five miles to a trading post. I think some arrangements were made to have the car towed back to Standing Rock, which was at least a hundred miles away. During all of the commotion, we got together with Jake Jr,. and boy, was he glad to see us. He was wearing a baseball uniform as he played on the team where Mother lived. The first thing I asked him was if there was anyone picking on him or wanted to fight him. He replied, "There were some guys who did that but now we are all friends."

We were trying to get home just before the Gallup Inter-Tribal Ceremonial. It was good to see our older sister and brother once we got back to Standing Rock.

We all went to the ceremonial together in Dad's pickup truck. We spent a few days and nights at the ceremonial. There was a large area set up as an Indian camp without fees to pay. Once we got squared away at camp I took off with my two younger brothers.

There were a lot of activities going on like Indian dances, games, foot races, wild horse races and the rodeo. We always had a lot of fun and when we got tired we came back to camp. I also got to see some of the students from the dorm. Brother and I got our cowboy boots along with a set of western clothes to wear to the ceremonial.

Many families from the Navajo reservation worked on farms in different states during the spring and summer months. Some of the families worked on the farms from planting until harvest time. They returned home early August to attend the ceremonial and put their children back in school.

I learned how to drive Dad's pickup truck while we lived at Standing Rock. You used the clutch to shift gears. At first, when Dad and I we were starting off, the pickup truck would jerk before it finally ran steady. After several tries and getting the feel of the clutch I was able to take off with less jerking. I learned to drive Dad's pickup truck on the dirt road that went from the camp to the trading post. Sometimes, Dad would let my two younger brothers and me take Grandma and an aunt to the Standing Rock trading post, where Grandma or Auntie would buy us boys a bottle of soda pop along with a candy bar. Eventually I learned more about driving and each time I got a chance to drive farther. I always enjoyed driving up into the mountains where the families in the community got their firewood. Driving on the reservation, I needed to learn quickly how to drive in muddy and snowy conditions.

Starting my eighth grade school year meant I had to attend Gallup Junior High where there were only eighth and ninth graders in attendance. This school was larger than the last school I attended and classes were held in different buildings. My classes included wood and metal shop along with an art class.

In my shop classes I got a chance to learn about and use different power tools. The power tools were used to cut wood or metal. During this time, I was able to make small class projects that I took home.

In my wood shop class I made bookshelves, bookends, picture frames and a small jewelry box. In my metal shop class I was first introduced to welding equipment. I learned how to use a gas welder and the electric welder. I got to like using both welders so I helped other students when they needed some help. I did this because some of the guys were afraid to use the welders. In my art class I enjoyed working with watercolor and oil paints. I was able to paint several pictures. My favorite was painting landscape scenes of northwest New Mexico – the flats, mountain ranges, the red rocks, always with some livestock in the picture.

During the physical education class there were different required activities. Some of these activities were bowling, gymnastics, wrestling and dancing. I was kind of shy so I did not like the dancing portion. When it was time to select a dancing partner I pretended I was running off. One time a chaperone ran after me and caught up with me. I had to dance with her for the remainder of the class. The dancing class turned out okay after I learned how to dance the right way.

I enjoyed my bowling class as it was held at one of the local bowling alleys. We were each fitted with bowling shoes and instructed on how to choose a bowling ball. Starting off I kept throwing the ball toward my right side, straight into the gutter. After doing this several times I asked my teacher, Mr. Anderson, for help. He told me what I was doing wrong. He suggested that I be in a different position when I released the ball. Much to my surprise this did the trick. My performance improved and I was having fun.

The other two activities I enjoyed were wrestling and gymnastics. In the wrestling class we had an intramural tournament according to our weight. I surprised myself by winning my weight division. The championship rounds for each weight class were held at the high school. We did our competition before the high school's regularly scheduled meet with another school. After we got done we got a chance to watch the high school wrestlers in action.

In the gymnastics class we had to complete an obstacle course. The course was hard to maneuver at first. After several tries and learning how to maneuver correctly I managed to complete it successfully. I realized that becoming a good wrestler or a good gymnast required hours of practice and being aware of one's position at all times. Shop and physical education were fun but we also had the academic courses that needed to be learned. I had good teachers at this school as they were always there for their students.

While attending Gallup Junior High I tried out for

the Wildcat track team and made it as a long distance runner. A couple of my friends from the dorm, Dave and Nelson, also made the team. Together we were able to travel to different schools to participate in track meets. During our school's invitational track meet it felt kind of strange to be competing against my former classmates from Crownpoint. It turned out to be fun after all to be with these guys. One of them asked, "What are you doing here?"

I replied, "I have moved away from Crownpoint and ended up here."

"Do you live in town?"

"I stay at the dorm when I attend school."

"So where do you really live?"

"I live at Standing Rock," I answered.

When school let out for the usual holiday breaks I would go back to Standing Rock to help Dad and other relatives. I also made an effort to visit Mom for a few days. This way I got to know my two little sisters, Cynthia and Jolene, a little better. During Thanksgiving and Christmas I went over to the Standing Rock chapter house to enjoy the holiday dinners provided for the community. I took Grandma Bess and a couple of aunties, so they could enjoy dinner and visit with relatives. There I got a chance to meet my other relatives and make new friends.

There are chapter houses situated throughout the Navajo reservation, which is sectioned off by region. There community governmental planning and management take place. Each chapter consists of three officers elected by the community to help govern the community. There are also small elected groups to assist the three elected members. The chapter house is utilized by the community members for various events, providing that you are a registered voter. Several of my aunties and uncles served as elected tribal officials over the years. I remember that Dad served on the Standing Rock school board for many years.

By now I was old enough to work with other students at the chapter house for the summer. As student workers we put together fundraising events to raise money for a cookout. We wanted to have a large cookout and invite the community members. One event I remember was a country and western dance with a live band. This event brought in a good amount of money to help us. Like always, something out of the ordinary took place; in this case it was drinking and fighting. We managed to make enough money to have our cookout for the chapter officials and the community.

Working there allowed us to help some community members, especially our elders and those less fortunate. We did some minor home repairs like painting, replacing broken windows and small roof repairs. We also did a good amount of chopping firewood, as most of us used firewood for cooking and heating. We also did some livestock corral repairs where they were needed. Most of the materials for repairs were donated by the chapter house. I think the students enjoyed helping others and at the same time, learned from doing it. We had a chapter-elected supervisor who had work skills to do these repairs correctly. Each time we completed one of these jobs, the occupants living there were thankful. Sometimes, they prepared a meal for us to show their appreciation. I always enjoyed eating some fry bread and chili beans.

During our breaks and our lunch time we went to the trading post to hang out with the trader, Mrs. Billson. She was a non-native American and a very helpful person who cared about the people of the community. She kept her trading post well-stocked with the necessities we needed. I attended school with a couple of her boys, Richard and Lance. Over time I became good friends with these guys. I remember trying to teach them some words in Navajo. We always got a kick out of doing that but one of them was determined to learn some.

Sometimes, we workers pitched in to buy some bologna, bread, cheese, chips and soda pop for lunch from the trading post. The girls would always have money as, I think, they took life more seriously than most of us did.

From the Standing Rock chapter, going east or west, there are chapters an hours' drive away. Each chapter put a softball team together consisting of both the girls and boys working there. One summer, Jerry and I worked at the chapter house at the same time. The softball team selected him to be our pitcher. We had a good team and won some of our games. One time after a western dance at our chapter house, our team and the team from another chapter got into a fight over an earlier game.

I got a chance to work at the chapter house for a couple of summers. It was an opportunity for us to learn about work ethics, money management and other responsibilities.

The program was sponsored by a Navajo tribal youth program. I saved some of the money I earned and used the rest to buy food and my school clothes. During the school year I worked part time at one of the restaurants, washing dishes, so I could have spending money. I think I learned to provide for myself at an early age.

Completing my eighth and ninth grade years at this school meant that I had to move on to Gallup High School. This school had students in the tenth, eleventh and twelfth grades. That meant hundreds of students filling the hallways between classes. On my first day at Gallup High I felt great, knowing that I was attending one of the bigger schools in New Mexico. I had been there before but only to the gym and the front lobby. Back then I noticed the lighting in the gym was different from other gyms I had seen.

I had to take several classes, both required ones and electives. I wanted to take a course in auto mechanics and in auto body repair. I found out the class was full to capacity with a waiting list. Instead I took wood shop as an elective during my tenth grade year. My first semester I made a coffee table out of mahogany. My second semester I made a dresser with four drawers, also out of mahogany. I was allowed to take these projects home after paying for the material used.

In the metal shop class I made a basketball goal just like the real thing except smaller in size. I took the goal home put a net on it and set it up. I enjoyed playing ball with my brothers and cousins. Sometimes, we played girls against boys. The goal remained up for several years until one day I noticed it was gone. I also did a good amount of welding in my metal shop class. Another elective I enjoyed taking was vocational agriculture. The Future Farmers of America (or FFA)

71

was a part of this class. The class was divided into two sections with a lecture session and shop time. There, I did more welding and helped a student named Lester make a metal toolbox for a pickup truck. The students in this class helped construct some rough-stock bucking chutes on some donated property at the edge of town. Those chutes were made to let the high school rodeo club practice rough-stock riding.

I took the required courses and was not all that interested in them but still made good grades. During the evening hours after dinner at the dorm we had study hall. Some of the teachers came to the dorm to provide tutoring sessions, which helped me to gain a better understanding of what was being taught.

For Bengals sports there was too much competition in football, basketball and wrestling among the students. I stayed with running long distance and ran cross country and track for the school. I got a chance to travel to other big schools in the state.

During my high school years I continued to stay at the dormitory during the school months. I went home during the holidays, summers and sometimes for the weekend. While staying at the dorm, I learned what it meant to be independent and responsible for myself. I remember that staff members reminded us that this would help us later in life.

Wanting to do something different, I started looking for work away from Standing Rock. One summer I was invited by a friend named Willie to go to Idaho to work on a farm. While in Idaho, working in the potato fields, I did what I call "hard work." I helped with irrigation where we moved aluminum pipes across the fields.

Sometimes some areas were saturated and some of the pipes still had water in them. This made it extra hard to move the pipes and took extra time. Some people went there every summer to do this kind of work. I thought to myself at the end of the summer that those guys were probably in tip-top shape. When harvest came I had another adventure when I worked in a potato cellar where potatoes were stored.

I had never seen that many potatoes in one place at the same time. There were several large cellars where we worked. The potatoes were brought into the cellars by large ten wheeler trucks, similar to full-sized dump trucks. When the trucks came into the cellars, they turned around and backed up to unload potatoes onto a conveyer belt. We guided the conveyer belt from side to side to stack the potatoes evenly. After the trucks left the cellar, I jumped onto a small farm tractor. Using this tractor I moved the excess dirt and debris away. Sometimes, I would unexpectedly drive the tractor straight at my friend Willie, trying to scare him. Here, I learned how to drive and operate the farm tractor and also tried driving one of those large ten wheelers when a driver had time to show me. Most of the drivers were young college-age adults and several were female drivers. After a day of stacking potatoes, I grabbed me a few to take back and fry. I liked those potatoes with some Indian tortillas. During this time some of my relatives and friends were also working nearby, which made it feel like home. We went there to visit or to get some Indian tortillas. This was an adventure for me as it was definitely something different.

Near the conclusion of my tenth grade year I was

into weight lifting with some friends. One night at the dorm, wanting to get in a work out before going to bed, I started lifting. There was something always going on at the dorm like music, watching television or guys swapping stories. I was doing some arm curls, standing, facing my bed which had a metal frame. I don't know what happened but I blacked out, then fell forward.

I guess I hit the bunk bed frame first, then hit the floor with my face. My friend Herman ran up to me, then took off to get the night attendant, Mr. Noble. I slowly got up with the help of my friend and the night attendant. We went to the bathroom so I could rinse out my mouth. When I put some water in my mouth I felt a sharp pain. The night attendant looked at me and commanded, "You need to get to the hospital right away."

I put on my clothes and we took off for the hospital. I kept my mouth closed, biting down on a clean cloth. When we got to the hospital the doctor took good care of me. Confused and concerned, the doctor stated, "We took out one tooth but I don't know where the other one is."

Mr. Noble, quickly replied, "Here it is. I went back to look around and found it on the floor."

The doctor responded, "You did a smart thing."

I did not attend school the next day because my face was swollen with a couple of teeth missing. There were two other students who got hurt and also lost a couple of their teeth in sports-related events that school year. I continued attending school and slowly got used to my missing teeth.

Attending this school I did not have as much interest

in activities like dances and proms. I hardly attended any of these activities. During this time, I checked out of the dorm, stating that I would be at the prom. Instead of going, however, I got together with some friends to do something else. I remember there were a bunch of girls and boys at this place out of town. When we got there everybody was drinking beer, talking and laughing. This went on for some time until people started to leave.

The activities I liked to attend were sporting events like football or basketball games and wrestling. A school bus came to pick us up at the dorm. A student who wanted to go had to sign up a couple of days earlier.

With nothing to do staying at the dorm during the weekend, I checked out of the dorm to go home. Sometimes I made it home and other times I ran into a cousin or a friend. We ended up doing something else besides going home. They would bring me back to the dorm on Sunday evenings. I usually had my homework completed and my laundry washed and ironed by Friday evening. I did this so I could have a free weekend, especially as a senior.

Chapter Four
Encountering Vision Problems

At seventeen, one cold winter day half way through my senior year, sitting in one of my morning classes, I was looking outside at some birds fighting over something. I noticed that my vision in my right eye suddenly became sort of fuzzy. Deeply concerned, I tried blinking and rubbing my eyes, but nothing happened. The weird thing about this was that I did not feel any physical pain but did feel a cold chill sweeping down my back. I then felt a bolt of fear rush throughout my body where I felt a sense of darkness.

I regained my awareness, and thought of waiting until after class to tell my teacher, Mrs. Allison, what was going on. After the bell rang, all the students quickly headed for their next class. I changed my mind about telling my teacher, and left the classroom as well. I thought it would be better to wait until tomorrow to tell anyone because I had an eye examination scheduled for that day. Walking to my next class with all the laughter, talking and other commotion in the hallways, I briefly smelled bread baking from the school cafeteria. I thought, wow, one of my favorites – school- made buns. It must be hamburgers and French fries for lunch today.

The next day I made it to my eye appointment downtown. During the examination, I told the optometrist, Dr. Taylor, that everything in my right eye was all fuzzy. He asked me if I had a doctor at the Indian Health Service hospital in town. I told him that I did and that I lived at the government dormitory in town. He quickly said, "I need to make a referral to the eye doctor at the Indian Health Service hospital."

I replied, "Okay," and waited around for him. I left Dr. Taylor's office after he made the referral and went back to the dorm.

A couple of days later one of the dorm attendants, Mr. Willie, took me to the hospital. The attendant asked, "What happened to your eye?"

I replied, "I really don't have any idea. My vision just got sort of fuzzy."

"Did you bump your head against anything?"

"I don't remember doing anything like that."

"Can you try to remember anything that could be helpful for the doctor?"

I said, "I recall one time when I was in the tenth grade, I had an accident lifting weights."

"What do you mean, an accident lifting weights? Can you tell me more about the accident?" he asked.

"I passed out doing some arm curls and fell forward flat on my face, hitting the floor and injuring my mouth."

"Wow, you must have hit pretty hard with the extra weight pulling you down."

"Yes, I had to go to the hospital late that night to be treated."

Just then he slowed down, as we turned into the hospital's crowded parking lot. He anxiously drove around looking for a parking space. Finally finding a space, he parked the car and turned off the motor and we got out and walked into the outpatient clinic area. Standing in line waiting to check in, he tactfully asked, "Does your eye hurt?"

"No, that's what is weird about the whole thing." I waited for what seemed like hours when suddenly I heard my name over the intercom. I must have dozed off sitting there because I was startled when I heard my name. Mr. Willie motioned, "Come on, buddy, we have to go up to the third floor to the eye clinic."

I replied, "Okay" and followed him. The elevator door was already open so we stepped in quickly and pressed the third floor button. Upward we went and in an instant the door reopened on the third floor.

I checked in at the front desk and was told to wait for a couple of minutes. Again I waited outside the eye clinic until my name was called, after which I walked into a dimly lighted room. I sat down in a chair near what looked like eye-examining equipment. The doctor approached me, placed his hand on my right shoulder and said, "Hello there, young man, how are you doing today?"

"Fine," I replied, "I was referred here by one of the local optometrists."

"Can you tell me what is going on?"

Nervously, I replied, "The vision in my right eye got sort of fuzzy all of a sudden the other day but I don't feel any pain."

Lifting my chin slightly, he said, "Here, let me take a look at it." Turning to his nurse, Nancy, he instructed, "Please put two drops from each bottle in his right eye. I need to get his eye dilated before I can examine it." Taking the small bottles from him she did so. Softly touching my shoulder the nurse asked, "Can you please step over this way and lie down on this table?"

Feeling kind of nervous, I stood up and walked over to the table, placing myself in the middle. I laid back on the table, stretching my legs out to the other end. I said, "Man, it sure feels good to lie down."

The nurse asked, "Please open your eyes for me so I can put the drops in." With her soft fingers she carefully kept my eyelids open while applying the drops with her other hand. "Now keep your eye closed so it can dilate and wait for the doctor."

"Okay," I agreed and laid there quietly, but deep inside I felt rather uneasy. She took hold of my right hand and placed a tissue there as she gently wiped the excess drops around my eye.

As I laid there on the table, wondering what the doctor was going to do, Dr. Smith came and stood on one side of the table with Nancy on the opposite side.

"Please open your eyes for me, young man, so I can take a look."

When I opened my eyes I noticed the room was darker than before. The doctor was wearing an instrument fastened around his head. At the front of this gadget was a small scoop-shaped lens with a light beam shining out. He said, "I am going to take a look at the back of your eye with this bright light so this might feel a bit uncomfortable. If it starts to hurt you let me know by raising one of your hands."

Just as I said, "Okay" I felt the bright light hit my eye and everything turned a reddish color. He kept moving around above my head, changing what I think was the lens. This went on for some time as I lay there, not making a sound. Turning to the nurse he asked, "Can you put some more drops in his eye, please?" I did not mind more eye drops as they sort of soothed the pain to where it was bearable. After what seem like an eternity, the examination was finally over.

Dr. Smith stated, "It is a good possibility that we are looking at a detached retina." I was puzzled so I asked him what that meant.

He explained, "There is a slight tear at the back of your eye where the retina is located."

"A detached retina, huh?" I repeated.

"Yes, because of this tear your vision is blurred."

"When I look at the window with my right eye it appears fuzzy, but when I look at it with my left eye, the window appears normal."

He waited until I finished, then informed me, "Correcting this tear may require eye surgery."

"Eye surgery?"

"Yes, but we don't have the specialist at this hospital."

"So, where would you refer me?"

"The nearest specialist is located in Albuquerque. I recommend the surgery be done as soon as possible."

I did not say anything, but instead just laid still,

thinking to myself, surgery, huh?

Then he spoke up again. "Considering that you are a minor we would need your parents' signatures to get permission before anything is done."

"Okay, but my parents are divorced. My mother Rita lives in Arizona, and my dad, Jack Sr., lives away from town on the reservation."

I gave Dr. Smith the necessary information that he needed to contact my mother or my father. He walked over to his desk, sat down, picked up the phone receiver, and dialed a number.

Talking to someone, he identified himself, "This is Dr. Smith, and I have a young man here who I just examined."

I heard what the doctor was saying, but of course could not hear the other person.

He continued, "My finding is a detached retina, but we need one of his parents' signatures before we can do anything."

Listening to the doctor while lying on the table, I felt fear slowly building up inside me, and at the same time I started drifting off into outer space.

Suddenly, Nancy jarred me back into reality as she said softly, "You can sit up if you like."

I sat up slowly and stepped onto the floor, then stood up noticing my breathing had slightly escalated. I started walking towards the chair to sit back down, wondering, what is going on with my eye?

"Come sit over here in this chair, young man," Dr. Smith directed me.

I sat down next to his desk, and Nancy asked, "How did you get to the hospital?"

"The dorm attendant brought me. He is waiting outside in the hallway."

She walked over to the doorway to take a peek. She looked at me and whispered, "What is his name so I can call him in?"

"Mr. Willie," I said, and gave her a brief description of him.

She went out the doorway, then brought him in and he sat next to me. Mr. Willie got close to my ear and whispered, "What's going on, partner?"

"They need a signature from one of my parents to get permission to do eye surgery," I whispered back.

Looking at me with his mouth half-way open, he then continued the whispered conversation, "Did you say, eye surgery?"

"Yes, eye surgery. You heard me right."

"Are you telling me that your eye is that bad?"

"I don't know, I guess it is."

He just sat there, looking at me, then at Dr. Smith.

"Dr. Smith told me that there is a small tear at the back of my eye where the retina is located." The distress was clear in my voice.

Before we left, Dr. Smith talked with Mr. Willie to explain my situation. Afterwards, Mr. Willie said, "I guess we can go now."

We walked back to the elevator, pressed the down arrow button, and waited there for a while. The elevator door opened up so we stepped in and went down. Coming out, I quickly glanced around the front lobby on the first floor, hoping to see a relative from home. I desperately wanted to get a message to my dad because he was not near a phone. Unfortunately, I did not see anyone I knew.

Continuing to walk, I looked outside and it seemed to be cold. I stepped through the front doorway of the hospital and started walking down the sidewalk. Looking down, I touched the handrail every now and then as I continued walking. I was thinking about whether or not my vision was going to return to normal when I reached the car. Mr. Willie unlocked the door on the passenger side and then opened it for me. I got in, sat down, and took one more look around for a relative.

I did not say too much on our way back to the dorm. We reached the parking lot and parked the car. As I was getting out, I thanked Mr. Willie, and started walking towards the stairway that led up to the second floor. Just then, my friend Tom came up and stopped me.

"Hey, dude, what happened at school today? I didn't see you during lunch, and no one knew where you disappeared to."

"Hey, dude, it's a long story. I'll tell you later, like maybe after dinner."

"Okay, I guess I can wait."

"I hardly ate anything for lunch, so I am starving."

"Starving, huh? You poor guy."

"I hope they have something good for dinner."

"We're having meat loaf, corn, mashed potatoes, gravy, and chocolate cake. I saw it on the menu."

"Good, I could eat like a horse."

"Like a horse, huh? Wow, that would be a lot to eat."

We walked to the bottom of the stairway and went up together. He kept glancing at me like he wanted me to say something.

Jokingly, I said, "Don't worry, I wasn't with your girlfriend. So, I'll see you later after I put away my stuff."

"Okay, dude. I will be waiting to go to dinner with you." He walked off, laughing.

I went over to where my bunk and locker were, opened my locker, and placed my stuff inside. It was about an hour before dinner, so I laid down on my bed and dozed off for about 30 minutes. When I dozed off, I dreamed about being back at home and helping my dad. He was building a small two-room house with some other people who I did not recognize. After waking up and sitting on my bed, looking downwards at my cowboy boots, I began wondering, what if that dream meant something?

Just then, the dorm attendant, Mr. Yazzie, shouted, "Hey guys, it's chow time."

I stood up and started walking towards the front door when Tom came up to me, he asked, "Hey, are you ready to eat like a horse?"

Later in the week, I found out that my mother had signed the papers, which were then forwarded to the local hospital. The dorm was notified, so one morning I was excused from class to go back to the hospital. My eye was still blurry and everything appeared abnormal. All the students got on their school bus to take them to their designated schools. After this I was alone in the empty dorm. The quietness felt kind of spooky, like someone was watching me from behind a locker. I waited around, checking everything next to my bunk, and made sure my locker was locked. While doing so, I heard Mr.

Jones, one of the attendants, over the intercom asking me to come down. I started to feel afraid because I knew I would be going somewhere alone for surgery.

I had never had any form of surgery before, so I did not know what to expect. I thought about my parents and sisters and brothers, wondering, what will I do without them? I started walking down the aisle, turned, and continued down the long hallway. I stopped for a moment just before reaching the stairway. I walked down the stairs and entered the front lobby where I met Mr. Jones.

"Good morning," he said, "are you ready to go over for your eye appointment?"

Slowly, I replied, "Good morning. Yes, I guess so."

"Come on, I already started up the car, so it should be nice and warm."

I walked through the front lobby door and glanced at the girls' side of the dorm, then at our side. The dorm looked different and felt empty when all the students were not there. I didn't like it; it was too quiet and I started to feel lonely.

After I got into the car, we backed up and started down the main street. I looked back toward the cafeteria as it slowly disappeared among the buildings. There was snow on the ground with cold blue skies; the streets had been cleared earlier. Again, I did not say too much while we drove through town toward the hospital. I noticed there was not a cloud in the sky, so the sun was shining extra bright that day. We pulled up to the hospital parking lot and found a parking space right away. I got out of the car and stood there, looking around for a family member to give me comfort. I felt alone and afraid. Hmm, an emotion I don't feel often, I thought. Was I daydreaming or was it some kind of fear building up inside me?

Just then, Mr. Jones spoke up, "Come on, let's go. It's almost time for your appointment." Startled, I did not say anything to him, just zipped up my jacket. I closed the car door and started walking as I looked down at my cowboy boots. I walked up the slightly sloped sidewalk and through the front door. I continued to walk toward the elevator where people were waiting for it.

One of the elevator doors opened up and about half of the people waiting got in.

"We will get the next one," Mr. Jones stated with a half-smile.

"Okay," I replied, and we got onto the next elevator as soon as it opened up.

"Second floor, please," a lady's voice said.

We started to the second floor where the door opened up and a pretty nurse got off. The elevator door closed and we continued up toward the third floor where Mr. Jones and I got out. We reached the eye clinic, and when we got there, I peeked through the doorway and lightly knocked on the door.

A nurse whose nametag said Vicky came to me and asked, "Hi, can I help you?"

"I have an appointment here today."

"What is your name?"

I told her my name and why I was there. She calmly said, "Wait here for a couple of minutes."

I whispered, "Okay," and stood there. When she returned, she explained, "A driver will be picking you up here in a few minutes, but Dr. Smith wants to see you first."

"A driver and the doctor, huh? Okay."

Doctor Smith came out and said, "Hello, there young man! How are you feeling today?"

Slowly, I replied, "I guess okay."

"I got all the forms signed by your mother at a hospital near her home."

It must be the Shiprock Indian Health Service hospital, I thought.

"Your mother was provided with all the necessary information that has to do with the surgery."

Hesitantly, I replied, "I guess everything is in order, huh?"

"Young man, are you ready for your plane ride to Albuquerque?" The nearest eye specialist was located in Albuquerque, New Mexico, about 130 miles away. The hospital had made arrangements for me to be flown there.

"Yes, probably as much as I could be."

"This could be fun," he said confidently.

"I've never been on a plane before."

"There will be two other patients flying with you, so don't be afraid."

"It's not the plane ride I am afraid of..."

"Not the plane ride? Then, what is it?"

I answered numbly, "It is my eye condition and the surgery. It frightens me."

With assurance he said, "The specialist you are going to is one of the best in the area."

"Is that right? Good, but I am still worried."

"Try not to be afraid."

Feeling anxious, I responded, "I bet when I get closer

to Albuquerque, I will be more worried than I am right now."

Just then, a gentleman came up to the doctor and said, "Hello, Dr. Smith, I am ready to take your patients to the airport."

"Okay, Mr. Morgan, I think this young man is ready to fly." Doctor Smith then turned toward me. "Good luck, young man, you will be fine."

"I hope so," I said as I smiled back at him and left.

I walked after Mr. Morgan, down the hallway and around the corner, not saying a word. He pressed the elevator down button and said playfully, "Down we go."

The elevator door opened up and we stepped in. He pressed the "G" button for "Ground Floor," then asked, "Going to Albuquerque, huh?"

I responded, "Yes, for eye surgery."

"Wow!"

Just then the elevator door opened and he stepped out, instructing me to "follow this way" as he turned toward a door that led outside. He held the door for me and we stepped outside into the cold, chilly air and started walking toward a car. He opened the passenger side door and I got in and sat down. Just then, another patient, Eddie, came and got in the back seat.

Cheerfully, he said, "Good morning, guys."

"Good morning, how are you doing?" I asked as Mr. Morgan positioned himself behind the steering wheel and started the car.

Mr. Morgan slowly backed out and took off toward the exit sign. He drove off down the street and kept going towards the airport located at the west end of town. On our way to the airport, we passed by the dormitory.

"Here is where I stay during the school year!" I was excited.

Mr. Morgan curiously asked, "So, where do you really come from?"

Proudly, I responded, "I come from Standing Rock, about fifty miles from here on the reservation."

"Here we are, guys, and there is your plane, ready to take off."

I got out of the car and walked toward the airport entrance. There was a man standing just inside the sliding doors who looked like he was waiting for us.

Mr. Morgan informed him, "Hey, Henry, here are the passengers who are going to fly with you today."

"Good. I am ready to take off, so let's go."

Henry started toward a door that led to the runway. Eddie and I followed him and walked to the small plane that stood there alone; I felt more afraid than before as I neared the plane. I approached the plane's entrance and looked inside through the little door.

The pilot, Billy, smiled. "Come on in and find a seat."

I got aboard and sat somewhere in the middle by a small window. We all fastened our seat belts and the plane started to move forward smoothly. Billy skillfully turned the small plane around and pointed it toward the runway. The engine started to idle faster as the plane took off down the runway. I don't know how fast we went, but all of a sudden the plane lifted off the ground. The engine kept racing and roaring as the little plane climbed upwards. I glanced at Billy and he had this unique expression with a big smile on his face. I interpreted the expression to mean he was pleased with himself. He turned the plane east toward Albuquerque as we seemed to level off.

Flying to Albuquerque, I got a good view from up above between Gallup and Albuquerque. Every now and then I glanced toward the north, thinking about home. There was a lot of snow everywhere. The diesel trucks cruising down the interstate did not appear as large as usual, but instead looked like toys. The mountain ranges also appeared small. The small towns had a different appearance compared to when I was on the ground. I don't know how far up we were but I think it was cold outside. The pilot had the heater running full blast. Every now and then it seem like we hit a bump and the plane bounced slightly, which felt weird. We made it to Albuquerque and landed safely where a car was waiting for us. The driver, Gilbert, took two other people to their destinations first. Then, after driving around for a while, it was finally my turn.

When we pulled into the hospital parking lot I started to feel the butterflies jumping around in my stomach. As my heart raced, I calmly felt a chill soothe my skin. I felt very alone; it was late in the afternoon and it was going to be dark soon. My mind slipped back to my childhood days, being with family and friends when I did not have any eye problems.

The day after arriving at the hospital I went in for eye surgery. The surgery was to repair the damaged retina. Doctor Allen gave me something that put me to sleep right away. I woke up all of a sudden with a big headache. I noticed both my eyes were covered with bandages and my right eye felt a bit sore. I moved my arms and cleared my throat lying in bed. Standing by, the nurse, Pat, asked, "How do you feel?"

"Okay, but I am thirsty."

She asked, "Would you like some juice to drink?"

I replied, "Yes, and it would be nice if it is cold." She left my bedside and later returned with some orange juice. Pat said, "Here we go; I will put the straw into your mouth so you can drink the juice." I replied, "Okay," and I felt the straw touch my lips. I positioned the straw with my hand and started drinking the juice. The juice was cold and tasted good. All of a sudden I became nauseous and vomited all over myself and the bed. Pat patiently said, "That's okay, don't worry; I'll get some help to clean this."

I laid there and I felt sick. I started to prop myself upward, a little, just then she quickly responded, "Please don't move." I laid still, trying not to move. She informed me, "Doctor's orders are for you to remain flat on your back and keep your head still."

"Okay, for how long?"

She added, "A nurse will be near you most of the time because you are not allowed to move."

I asked, "What about when I have to eat or go to the bathroom?" She continued, "Don't worry about anything; we will be here to help."

I spent several days in the hospital after the surgery lying flat on my back. I spent Christmas, New Years Day and my birthday. A couple of the patients, George and Juan, got visitors on Christmas day as their family brought them some goodies. I remember Juan shared some homemade hot tamales with us. I liked eating chili so this treat made my day. The day after Christmas I got a surprised visit. My brother Jerry, sisters Etta and

Gracie, and Dad came into the room. The first thing my family asked Dr. Allen was how the surgery went. They also asked him how long I would be in the hospital. I guess Dr. Allen talked to my family.

Jerry said, "There is a lot of snow back home."

I replied, "Is that right?"

He said, "Remember Satan's Pass?"

"Yes, what about it?"

"There are about two feet of snow through there."

"Wow, and you guys made it through?

"Yes, and I was the one driving," he bragged. "Before we left home I put some flat rocks in the back."

I replied, "Oh, okay, so you can have better traction in the snow and ice."

"Yes, I had to get by a bunch of stuck vehicles up the pass."

I reminded him, "You are always a good driver and you guys will get home safe and sound."

"Yes, I think the snow plows are out there clearing the roads just about now."

Just then one of the nurses, Carole, came in and said, "Can you excuse us for a second?"

Jerry responded, "Yes, of course."

"It is time for your eye drops," Carole said.

I replied, "Is that right?" She slowly lifted the bandages and placed the drops into my eye. Lying there, I tried to focus my eyes so I could take a look at her but she was only a blur.

She asked, "How are you doing?"

I cheerfully replied, "I am fine. My sisters, brother and my dad are here for a visit."

"That's great," she said. Then she slowly put new

bandages on my eyes. "I will see you later and check by before I go home."

"That sounds good," I responded. Carole was one of the nurses who I got closer to than the other nurses.

After she left, my family asked me if I needed anything from the store. I answered, "It sure would be nice to have a small transistor radio for some music."

Dad said, "I think we can all pitch in and get you one."

"That would be great -- I can listen to my country music." My sisters Etta and Gracie asked, "What about personal hygiene items?"

"I really don't need any. They have that here."

My brother Jerry asked, "What size radio were you thinking about?"

I replied, "A small one will do, with some extra batteries." After visiting and catching up on things at home, they left for the store. When they returned I got my radio, extra batteries and some Christmas candy. Before my brother Jerry left he gave me a stiff and solid hand shake and reassured me, "Hang tough." We usually used this term for a boost when one of us was going through some kind of turmoil. Feeling sad but at ease, my sisters Etta and Gracie said together, "We love you and hope you get well soon." In our native language, Dad spoke. "Keep your spirits and courage up; I will be praying for you."

I sadly replied, "Okay," then felt some tears forming underneath my bandages. I could hear their footsteps walking away, then disappearing down the hallway. I laid there, unable to move, with tears running from under my bandages. I felt instant loneliness; I was on my own again. Just then a nurse, Maria, came to my bedside and took hold of my hand.

Compassionately, she said, "I know it is hard on you." I could not say anything so I just gestured with my hand. "I am here and I will do my best to help you feel better," she reminded me.

New Year's Day came and went as well as my eighteenth birthday. On this day, the hospital kitchen baked me a small birthday cake. It was about five inches in diameter and about three inches high. Not wanting to eat it, I asked if I could keep it. They let me keep the cake next to my bed on a night stand. I wanted to take it home to show to my little brothers because I thought it was neat. The cake was special with all the decorations but it was a miniature one. The nurses who took care of me liked my little cake. One of them, Maria, said, "It is a pretty cake and is very small." She brought it to me so I could touch it to get a better idea. Surprisingly, it was very detailed with a couple of roses and expressions of Happy Birthday on it but sure enough, it was very small.

I continued to stay in the hospital flat on my back, not allowed to lie on either of my sides for several more days. I had to keep my head stable, facing upwards. Sometimes they kept a pillow on each side of my head to keep it from moving. I was fed three times a day lying like this. I also had some snacks and had to eat them the same way. It was difficult to swallow my food at first but the nurses knew how to make it easier. One day when a nurse named Mary came in she said, "Guess what?"

I asked, "What is it?"

She replied, "The doctor is letting you sit upright a little in bed." In disbelief I said, "Wow, this is great. Finally, I can start sitting up." She raised the bed a little, putting me in a slight incline and not flat like before. I admitted that it would make it easier to swallow my food.

She agreed. Eventually, I was allowed to sit upright for longer periods with more movement about the room. Sometimes, I would go walking down the hallway wearing a bandage on my right eye.

I was often reminded not to lean over too much. One day Larry, one of the patients in my room, fell off his bed. Without hesitation, we helped him to get back into bed.

I don't think we told anyone about this incident until the patient told it to a nurse himself. Later, I was allowed to go and visit another patient, Tommy, with the same eye condition.

While visiting him nurse Mary asked, "Would you like to help your friend with his snack?" I replied, "I'll be glad to help him only if it's okay with him." He responded, "Yes, that is okay with me." Afterward, I found out that this task was not easy to do.

One day in mid-January, my dad, my younger brother Steve and my cousin Henry came into my room. I asked Carole, one of the nurses who was working that day, if it was okay for me to go home. She replied, "As far as I know you can go but let me double check," and then walked off.

She came back and informed me, "The doctor needs to check your eye before you can go."

I replied, "Okay, but when?"

"Right now." The nurse and my cousin brother Henry carefully moved me onto a stretcher-like a bed with wheels. Carole connected the straps and tightened me in slightly. She pushed the bed out the room, then down the hallway. She teasingly said, "You don't really want to go home now, do you?"

I replied with mounting frustration, "I think it is time to go home because I am tired of being in one place everyday." We reached a room where Dr. Allen was and he took a look at my eye. To my disappointment, he said, "I am sorry but I don't think it is a good idea for you to go home right now."

With a sinking heart, I asked, "Why is that?"

"I am afraid that the surgery did not come out the way it should have," he replied. Suddenly, all of my memories and love of freedom rushed through me and I said, "I don't want to have another surgery."

"If you don't have this problem corrected, there is a good chance you will go blind in that eye."

"I just want to go home," I complained.

I got used to several of the nurses who worked at this hospital. A couple of them, Carole and Maria, who were working that day, asked me to stay until my eye problem was corrected.

I said, "My mind is made up to go home." Before leaving the hospital I had to sign some forms. I got the clothes that I had worn when I came to the hospital. Carole helped me get dress and it felt good to put on my clothes. She asked, "Are you sure you are doing the right thing?"

"I think I am."

With concern, she said, "Good luck. When you are

in the city, come by and visit us."

"I might come back for a visit one day," I replied. Before leaving, I was supplied with extra bandages and eye drops for my right eye.

The four of us walked out of the room and down the hallway. We took the elevator down to the first floor, then got off. We continued to walk to the hospital's front doors, then outside. Stepping outside, the first thing I felt was the cold winter air. I said, "Man, it's cold out here."

My younger brother Steve agreed, "Yeah, it is," as he walked next to me. My dad took care of some business in Albuquerque before leaving town. We headed for home and stopped along the way to grab something to eat. I was craving a hamburger so we stopped at a burger joint to have one. My cousin brother Henry said, "I think I'll take a couple of them home with me." These burgers were larger than what I was used to. I had mine with green chili which made it extra good. Turning toward my cousin I asked, "What are you going to do with those burgers?"

He replied, "I am going to eat one when I get home and take the other one to work."

The rest of us did not want any more, so we headed out down the road. We kept driving and I noticed the snow was getting deeper as we approached home. We arrived and I said, "It sure is good to be home." I never realized until that day how special this place would be to me from then on.

I stayed home, trying to take it easy, but at times started feeling restless. I went over to my Aunt Jean's house to check on her water supply and see if she needed some.

In our native language she cautioned, "You should not be doing any physical work, because you just came back from the hospital."

I responded, "I am okay and I promise not to overdo it." At this point, talking and understanding our native language had gotten better for me as well as for my brothers. I think my sisters knew how to speak more Navajo than us boys.

One day I returned to the dorm, only to find out I might have been dropped from school. This information was given to me by the dorm attendant on duty, Mr. Willie. I remember it was Sunday evening; I thought I would continue with school on Monday. I still had some of my clothes and school supplies in my locker. Standing there with the attendant I said, "I will check into this issue about school tomorrow."

He replied, "That would be a good idea."

I asked, "Would it be okay to stay here at the dorm tonight?"

He replied, "Yes, you are still considered a student here."

"That's great." I told my dad and sister Etta what was going on, saying, "I will let you guys know sometime tomorrow what happens at school."

My sister asked, "Do you want us to come over?"

"I don't think so, but if I need you guys I'll get a hold of you." She agreed as they were heading out to go home.

I returned to Mr. Willie to ask him about this issue about being dropped from school. "Who told you that I may have been dropped?"

He said, "Oh one of the other attendants."

I continued, "Did you guys get a letter from the school?"

He answered, "Not that I know of; you never know about these things."

I agreed, "Yeah, I think I know what you're talking about."

Reassuringly he said, "If I were you I wouldn't worry about it, because I know it will be resolved."

I replied, "Thank you for saying that, I feel better now."

The next day I got on the school bus as usual and took my usual seat. One of the guys, Ralph, sat next to me and jokingly said, "Hey dude, I have been taking care of your seat."

I asked with a grin, "Is that right?"

"Where have you been?" he queried.

"You don't know? I left for the hospital just before the Christmas break."

"Really? I had no idea."

"Yes, I had to have eye surgery."

"Wow, is that right?"

"Yes, but I'll be okay."

"Yeah, dude, just be tough and you will be all right." By this time all the students were on the bus and the bus started to move. Some of my buddies looked at me and smiled. So, I smiled back.

I got to the school and went straight to the principal's office. The secretary up front said, "Good morning, how can I help you?"

"Good morning, I'd like to talk with the principal,

Mr. Johnson."

She asked, "What is it about? Maybe I can help you."

"I have been away from school due to an emergency and now I am returning."

"Okay," she said, "but it will be a few minutes. Someone is with him right now."

"That's okay; I'll wait." I sat in the lobby until my name was called.

When I went into Mr. Johnson's office, he said, "Good morning, how can I help you?"

I replied, "Good morning, sir, I have been out of school because I needed eye surgery."

He said, "Okay, hold on," and called the guidance counselor, Mr. Guy, to his office.

I sat there while the two went over my school records. The principal said, "Go ahead and start attending your classes. Have each teacher sign this paper for you, then return it." I asked, "Does this mean I did not get dropped from school?"

Confused, he asked, "What do you mean?"

"When I returned to the dorm," I explained, "one of the attendants told me I might have been dropped."

"No, not at all, but you will need to do some catch up work."

"That will not be a problem."

"Your grades are good enough for you to continue with school," he said reassuringly."

"That's great," I responded. Leaving the principal's office, I went to my locker to take out some books and notebooks to use. It felt good to open my locker, yet sort of weird. Refocusing, I hurried to my first class and walked in just as the bell rang. I walked up to the teacher's desk and said, "Good morning, Mrs. Teller."

She smiled and replied, "Good morning, welcome back."

"I am glad to be back." I gave her the paper I got from the principal. She looked it over, signed it, and returned it to me. "I would like to meet with you after class," she said.

I cheerfully answered, "Okay," then went to find my chair where I used to sit. I quickly glanced around the classroom and it seemed like everyone was staring at me. Ella, the girl sitting behind me, poked me in the back and whispered curiously, "Hey, where have you been?"

I whispered back, "I'll tell you later on."

"I guess I can wait," she mumbled. Throughout the day, several of my friends and teachers asked me what happened and whether I was going to be okay.

I had mixed feelings about myself since my eye surgery. So, I did not try out for the track team like I did the previous years. I enjoyed running long distance as it gave me a sense of freedom and being in harmony with myself.

Instead of being one of the runners, I tried to compensate by watching the local track meets, but somewhere along the line I lost interest. There was still time to play some basketball or softball for the dorm, but I thought I would not be able to perform to my full ability. I think at this point I started to lose interest in sports and felt emotionally and physically drained. Peaks of reality were surfacing.

I continued to go to the hospital to have my eye

checked because the blurriness had gotten worse. During one of my visits I was informed that the eye surgery was unsuccessful and I would go blind in my right eye. When I got this information I started to wonder whether my left eye was going to be all right. I didn't know what I should be feeling or how to act. Was I supposed to be sad or angry? I think I was in a state of denial or maybe even in shock. I managed to continue to do everyday things but with some difficulty at first. I often felt frustrated and ashamed of seeing out of one eye. It would hurt but eventually, I slowly got used to seeing out of one eye. If I needed to turn around I turned toward my left side. If I turned toward my right side I would always bump into something or someone. When I bumped into someone either I felt embarrassed or that individual got upset. He would say something like "Why don't you watch where you're going?"

I learned that my left eye had to adjust to different things, especially judging distance. In time, I got used to seeing only out of my left eye. I recall talking with this guy Earnest with the same eye condition.

He confidently stated, "When you lose your sight in one eye then your good one seems to get better over time." At this point in my life I did not feel as ambitious as I once did; instead I started feeling a loss.

I completed all course requirements and became eligible to graduate despite of my eye condition. On graduation day several guys and girls got together and pitched in to get some beer and food. We all took off to a place out of town to have some fun. Some of the girls and boys cooked a bunch of hamburgers and hot dogs. We were all having a good time and sort of lost track of time. One of the girls, Linda, boldly stated, "Hey, you guys, I think we should be getting back to get ready for our graduation." The plan was to continue the party after the graduation. Some of the girls packed all the food and took it with them. Some of the boys packed all the beer and took it with them. I caught a ride back into town with one of the boys to where I was staying. Later, one of my friends from home, William, came by to pick me up to take me to the graduation. When we turned toward the high school the traffic was backed up to where a policeman was directing traffic. I told one of the police officers that I needed to get to the high school so he made room for us. We drove by several cars and made it to the high school parking lot. When I got there the tail end of the graduates were almost all in the gym. Both of my parents, my sister Etta and some friends attended my graduation. My older brother Jerry could not make it because he was in the military.

Drinking beer and goofing around earlier, I did not feel like doing a whole lot after graduation. I decided to go home to Standing Rock.

My ambition after high school was to join the military. This had to change immediately because of my eye condition. I felt cheated and left out because of not being able to serve my country like my brother, cousins and friends. Instead, I thought about learning some skills to be able to do automotive repairs. I was more interested in attending a vocational school rather then a college or university. Still worried and wondering what would actually happen down the road, I tried to stay focused and keep my self-confidence.

Chapter Five
Vocational Training

One fall day I left my home environment of the Navajo Reservation after having a busy summer. My ambition after high school was to join the military. This had to change immediately because of my eye condition. Instead I thought about learning some skills to be able to do automotive repairs. I was more interested in vocational training rather than a college or university. I boarded the Greyhound bus in Gallup one evening and rode the bus all night long. I was on my way to northern California to fulfill my automotive repair ambitions. I met a pretty Navajo girl on the bus as we sat together and talked. She had to change buses the next morning. I asked her for her address so I could write her a letter so we could remain in contact. Before she left she gave me her address. She was on her way back to school in Southern California.

I continued traveling northward most of the day. I reached my destination in the early evening hours. I felt lost and sort of scared because the city was very large. I already missed home and felt very lonely. I started thinking about what my dad told me to do in case I felt afraid. This was to remember that I am a Native of this land so I should use my traditional ways.

Arriving at the bus station, I noticed a bunch of taxi cabs parked out side. I claimed my luggage and approached one of the taxis. The driver spoke, "Here, let me help you with that luggage."

He took the luggage from my hands. I stated, "I need to get to the hotel around here some place."

He replied, "Okay we'll find it; come on." I got in the taxi and showed him the paper with the address. He said, "Okay I know where it is; besides that I take people there all the time."

We drove through traffic and suddenly pulled up in front of a large tall building. I thought to myself, "this is a very large hotel compared to those back home." The driver said, "I'll get your luggage for you; just go in through that door over there." I replied, "Okay" and got out of the taxi.

I walked into the lobby of this large hotel with a high ceiling, looking side to side. I noticed where I thought the front desk was and walked in that direction. I approached the desk and the person there said, "Can I help you?"

I answered, "Yes, I think I am supposed to stay here tonight." I pulled a folded paper out of my back pocket and showed it to him.

He assured me, "You are in the right place."

I replied, "Great!" Just then the taxi driver brought in my luggage. I paid him the fare and thanked him. I got squared away with getting my room for the night. The desk clerk said, "I'll have someone help you with your luggage here shortly."

One of the hotel workers took my luggage and showed me to my room. When I was alone in the room, the first thing I did was go over to the window to look outside. I almost fell over when I saw how far up I was. I tried to relax but had some difficulty, which may have been because of being in a large city.

I managed to get little sleep that night in the hotel. The sirens echoing through the tall buildings every now and then scared me.

The next morning, after a crazy and sleepless night I got myself all ready to go. I was wondering what I had gotten myself into by leaving the good old reservation. I took my luggage and stumbled down to the first floor where I met the hotel worker. Much to my surprise, he already knew what to do with me. He knew where I needed to go. So after breakfast, he called a taxi. I needed to get to the Bureau of Indian Affairs office.

I waited around until the taxi driver arrived. He said, "Here, let me help you with your luggage."

I replied "Okay" and followed him through the door.

He asked, "Where to, my friend?" I showed him the paper I had in my pocket. He replied, "Okay, let's go." I got in, sat down, and glanced up and down the street. The taxi ride seemed endless. Finally arriving, the driver spoke, "Here we are." As I got out of the taxi, I noticed a bunch of vehicles with government license plates parked in the parking lot.

I walked into a fairly large building where I noticed some Native American paintings hanging on the wall. I was greeted by some Native Americans at the office, so I felt at ease. One of the vocational counselors, Mr. Roberts, assisted me in getting situated. He helped me with where I was going to live during my training. I was going to stay at a boarding house. Here I would be getting a room and two meals a day in return for a rental fee and doing small chores around the house. While living in the dorm back at home, I had learned good housekeeping skills and here they would pay off. I arrived at the boarding house sometime during the afternoon hours and got myself settled in my room.

I stayed in the room until it was time for dinner. I walked downstairs and much to my surprise, there was Billy, a former classmate from school, sitting at a table. I approached the table and whispered, "Hey dude, is there anyone sitting here?"

He looked up and happily said, "No, go ahead and sit down." I pulled out the chair and sat down. He asked, "Wow, man when did you get here?"

I replied, "I got to the big city late yesterday."

He responded, "I got here earlier in the week and did some sightseeing."

I asked, "Did you see anything good?"

He replied, "Yes a bunch of pretty girls with different color hair."

We got our dinner and afterwards we helped the lady with some of the cleaning in the dining room. My friend Billy said, "Hey, let's go hang out in the other room?"

"Yeah, let's go; there's nothing to do right now," I replied. We talked a little about what type of training we were going to do.

It was Friday evening and I wanted to look around

the place this weekend. Looking at my buddy, I said, "I wish I could check out the city a bit."

He said, "If you like, I can show you where to catch the right street bus."

"Do you know where the training place is located?" I asked.

He replied, "Yes, I went over there today to take care of some paperwork."

I added, "Maybe tomorrow you can show me where this place is," I suggested.

"Yeah, that won't be a problem," he continued. "All you need to do is study this map; right here it will show you all you need to know."

Later in the evening we decided to go over and check out one of the clubs nearby. I thought maybe we would run into some Indian people from other tribes. We did see some Indians there at the club but did not bother them.

We hung around there for a while and drank some beer. There were a couple of Navajo guys, Ned and Tom, there drinking beer and playing pool. One of them approached us, wanting to tell us something. In our native language he said, "You guys need to be careful being in this big city. Where are you guys staying?"

I replied, "At a boarding house."

He responded, "Yeah, I know where it's at; I used to stay there when I first came here." After visiting and talking in Navajo with these two guys we left the club and went back to our new home.

I felt a little more at ease after finding a familiar friend here and talking with those guys. I told Billy that Id see him in the morning so he could show me where the training site was located.

Monday morning came and I made it to the training site. I got there by riding one of the early morning street buses. When I arrived at the training center, there were a bunch of students hanging around outside. I was looking for the front door; just then I spotted it. I went in and looked around in the lobby. I asked a person standing nearby if he knew where the office was. He gave me the directions and pointed toward a hallway. I walked down the hallway and came upon an open door where some students were standing in line.

I got in line and as I stood behind the last student in line, I asked, "Is this where we are supposed to check in?"

He replied, "Yep, you came to the right place."

"Thanks, I said, and then stood there then looking down at my cowboy boots. He asked, "Are you taking training here?"

"Yes, for auto mechanics."

"Is that right? So am I."

I said, "That sounds good."

He asked, "Where do you come from?"

I replied, "From the Navajo reservation in New Mexico; what about you?"

"From Alaska," he said.

"Wow, when did you get here?" I asked

"Last week by airplane, what about you?"

"I got here last Friday after a long bus ride." Just then it was his turn to go check in. After he got done I went in and took care of my paperwork. I walked out of the office and found my new buddy, Jack, waiting outside.

"Are you going to see the instructor today or later?" he asked.

"I think I'll go now since I am already here."

"That sound good; I'll go over with you."

We walked out of the building and across the street to another large building. We went in and located the instructor's classroom. We went inside, where a man in coveralls was sitting behind a desk with a big smile. He spoke, "Hello, there men! What can I do for you?"

"We are new students, taking auto mechanics."

"Let me check your papers to see if you men are in the right place," he offered.

We handed him our papers, and after looking them over, he replied, "Good, you are in the right place. Now take this paper with you to get your equipment."

"What about the textbook?" I asked.

"You will get it when class starts in a few days."

Jack and I left the room and stopped outside in the hallway. I asked Jack, "When are you going to pick up your equipment?"

"I don't know, what about you?"

"I have an idea," I replied. "We should go back and let Mr. Roberts, our counselor, help us out."

"That's a good idea," Jack agreed. "I think he will help us."

We walked down the hallway and out of the building. We continued to the bus stop and waited for the next bus, which dropped us off near the counselor's office.

Once there, we signed in and waited for our turn to see him. When he called one of us we both went in. He asked "What can I do for you guys today?"

We told him we were all set for training but needed

to pick up some equipment for the shop portion of the class. He stated, "I still have to meet with a couple of students; how about after lunch?" We agreed to come back after lunch and walked over to a hot dog stand around the corner for chili dogs and a drink. We went back to the counselor's office and found him ready to go.

He said, "Come on, guys – let's go get your equipment." We followed him out the door to one of the cars with a government license plate. We all got in and took off down the street, cruising with the windows open. The counselor said, "I hope you guys don't mind – I'm not too crazy about air conditioners."

We replied, "That's all right." We drove for a while and then pulled up in front of a large building. We all got off and went inside, where a store clerk met us. I gave him the paper I got from the auto mechanics instructor.

The clerk said, "Yes, I can help you with this stuff; just follow me." Before we took off he asked, "What about you two?"

My friend said, "Here is my paper."

The counselor added, "Not me – just the two of them."

The store clerk said, "Okay, then, let's go." We got our equipment and put it in the car. The counselor asked, "Where are you guys staying?"

"At a boarding house over on Alameda Street."

"I can take you back to where you guys are staying," he suggested.

We replied, "That would be great."

He added, "That is where most of our guys start off,

and from then move on."

In a couple of days I returned to the training site to start training. The rest of the new students and I toured the shop. I smelled the automotive repair shop hitting me when I took my first tour. I was excited, especially when I saw all the different tools and equipment used to do minor or major repairs. There were several engines blocks bolted to engine stands in one section of the shop. One engine stood out because one of the advanced students, Harry, told me he was working on it.

He said, "Hopefully I can fix it without it costing too much."

I asked, "What going on with the engine?"

He said, "The problem with this engine is that the guy who owns it took it apart all wrong."

"All wrong, huh? What does that mean."

"He did not specifically mark the parts like he was supposed to."

"So are the engine parts all mixed up?"

"Yes, they are," Harry said. I thought, wow, this is interesting. Like any normal kid, these guys brought their hot rods to work on, to make them run faster and sound powerful. While doing this they learned about auto mechanics, fixing their own cars. I felt uncomfortable because these guys had their own cars to work on and I did not have one. In class I met Peter, a Native American student from a different tribe. He let me help him work on his car and that relieved some of my discomfort. Sometimes after class I went cruising with him. He was used to the California lifestyle and had no problem driving. The traffic was always busy and there were many highway lanes to keep track of.

There was a good amount of information to be learned about auto mechanics. This was anything from the different types of screwdrivers to engine specifications. I learned that there was probably a tool for every auto repair that had to be made.

I did a lot of reading from different books. The repair manuals showed diagrams and pictures of the auto parts. Each make or model of automobile had its own repair manual along with its own specifications. Anyone could specialize in a certain area – like front end repair, brake repair, engine overhaul or engine tune-ups. One day my instructor, Mr. Wilson, said, "You should specialize in four-wheel-drive repair."

"Really?" I asked.

"That is the next big thing in pickup trucks, coming on real soon."

"That makes a lot of sense, because most of the people back on the reservation drive pickup trucks." I attended classes on a regular basis trying to learn as much as I could.

I kept thinking about what the instructor told me about four-wheel-drive pickup trucks. To be able to learn all that there was to learn about that would be great.

When there was time or money I went sightseeing with someone in this big city along the ocean. When I looked at the ocean I felt fear slowly building up in me. I often wondered why I felt this way when I got close to the ocean. I never told anyone about this while in California. I also went to a nightclub where a bunch of Native Americans hung out. I met several people there and most of them I did not see again. Here, I drank beer and played pool with a couple of friends. Once in a while I came across someone from the reservation. They were either attending training or were in the military. For some reason the girls would always save the day. Just like the day when, out of the blue, two Indian girls, Marilyn and Jennifer, who I had attended high school with, came walking down the street. It was great to see these girls, so I hung around with them for a while.

Once when I was walking down the sidewalk with some friends I saw a scene that I will never forget. A black gentleman came walking down the sidewalk dressed up in western clothes. He had on a pair of big black boots. Strapped to his boots were a pair of spurs that jingled with each step. A big black cowboy hat that could have easily been ten gallons covered his head. I don't know if he was a real cowboy but he looked to be pretty raunchy. When he approached, he did not say a word; he just stared straight ahead and walked by. I turned around to take another look at him and thought to myself. Man, this guy looks pretty wild. I don't know, it may have been a movie scene but it was very interesting. This caught my attention because I grew up with Jackson, a black kid back in Crownpoint. He would always say that he was part Indian and did the things we did.

This friend of mine would always wear a cowboy hat and cowboy boots. I remember one time I went to a squaw dance with him and his mother Bertha. His mother kept asking me questions about the squaw dance. I answered what I could and told her I did not know that much about it. We stayed there for a while and I think his mother fell asleep. My friend and I went walking around and ran into some buddies there. They asked us if we wanted some cigarettes or chewing tobacco. My friend whispered, "Sorry boys, not tonight, we're with Mom."

During my training I was sent to the hospital for an eye examination. The doctors at the hospital told me that I had a cataract in my left eye. Doctor Patterson said, "You probably need surgery to remove the cataract." I did not like the idea of having eye surgery again, especially this far away from home. I refused to have any kind of surgery. Once again I felt that bolt of fear rush through out my body that I did not like. I started feeling anxious.

I tried to concentrate on my training. As time went on I started to lose interest in being there. I think this was because I was feeling fear about my eye. I kept thinking, what if something bad happens to my eye? As time went on, I managed to pull myself back together and continue training.

In spite of what the doctor said, I wanted additional training to be able to increase my automotive repair skills. I wanted to learn about auto body repair and paint. I thought of doing some auto body repair training somewhere in Utah or Colorado. I did not complete my training there. I learned to be able to do some auto repair work, but I did not want to stay in California any longer.

I decided to pack my luggage and go home soon. I told a couple of my friends, Billy and Freddie, what I was going to do. They told me I should stay and at least complete my training. I told them I had made up my mind about going home.

Leaving California, I returned to Standing Rock and stayed with Dad. I helped him haul building materials to build a new home. We drove about 100 miles a day for the building materials. There were a group of men who were going to build the new house. When I was home I helped these guys with whatever I could.

I was afraid to go to my counselor, Mr. Neilson, at the government education office. I knew I had to tell him sooner or later that I had discontinued my training. One day I had enough courage built up to go and face him. I borrowed my dad's pickup truck and drove to Crownpoint. I got to the building where the office was located and waited outside in the pickup for a while. Building up my courage again, I finally got out and went inside. I was walking down the hallway just then he came walking toward me.

I stopped and said, "Hello there, sir." He looked at me twice then asked, "Is that really you?"

I said, "Yes it is really me."

He added, "Are you here to see me?"

"Yes, sir."

"Go ahead and wait in my office; I will be back right away."

I got to his office, found a chair and sat down; my stomach started tying itself in knots. I tried to remain calm but it seemed to get worse. I heard footsteps coming from down the hallway. I thought it was probably him. Sitting there, I kept wondering, *how should I tell him what happened?* and just then he walked in. I glanced at him, then looked downwards. He asked, "How are you doing today?"

"Okay. I came to tell you about my training."

"I already know what you are going to tell me."

"Is that right?"

"Yes, I get a report on everyone attending training under this program."

"Did I jeopardize my chances for any future training?" I asked nervously.

"Right now we would have to suspend you until further notice," he replied.

"Okay. I thought it would be best for me to come in and talk to you."

"Yes, I am glad you did."

I went on, "I guess I'll be on my way if there is nothing else."

He answered, "When I find out anything about your case, I'll contact you by mail."

Uneasily, I agreed, and left the office. Eventually, my suspension was lifted and I was eligible to try again. I went back to the office and submitted an application to train for auto body repair. I made two choices for location and was accepted in central Utah.

One fall day I left home again to attend training, this time in Utah. I arrived in a small town by bus in the late afternoon. The small town in south-central Utah seemed like farming and ranching lands. I liked this small town because it was situated in the valley among some huge mountains with a lot of fresh air and open space. After arriving I stayed in a motel that already had reservations for me. This small town was great compared to a large California city. The next day I met with the vocational counselor, Mr. James, who came from Arizona. Again, just like the counselor in California, he helped me get my living and training situations organized. I was provided with a bi-weekly stipend to pay for my living expenses during training. Coming here, I did not feel as lonely as I did when I first arrived in California.

I rented an apartment with two Navajo students from the reservation, Tony and Edward. The three of us living together helped ease expenses. We pitched in three ways for rent and groceries, rather than paying individually. We took turns cooking, washing dishes and keeping the place clean. We took care of our own expenses like personal care items. Of course, there were times we got into our arguments, especially after we had been drinking at the local beer joint. We still looked out for one another because that is the Indian way.

Living in this small town, transportation to school was a lot easier. It was walking distance compared to California. When I got to know some of the local students one of them gave me rides back to my apartment.

The training site was adjacent to a high school. We shared the cafeteria with the high school students. I had lunch at the cafeteria as it only cost 35 cents. Some of the high school students took either auto mechanic or auto body training with us. I noticed that this training center had both kinds of training in one place.

I kept thinking to myself that I should have come here first. In California the two types of training were located at two different places.

Reporting for the first day of class was exciting for me as we met in the classroom. The classroom was right next to a big auto body shop. I got my textbook, coveralls and some hand tools. The instructor, Mr. Hayes, seemed to be a nice person with a good sense of humor. I introduced myself as did the rest of the students. All the new students took a tour of the shop and the painting room. Next we were introduced to all the hand tools, hydraulic tools and air power tools used in the shop. There were some vehicles parked in the shop that were being worked on by the advanced students. The rest of the day we were allowed to watch the advanced students working on their vehicles.

The next day I got my first project from my instructor when he gave me an old car door to repair. This was after he banged it up with a pipe. I still remember the color, which was a dirty blue with a chrome strip running down the middle.

He instructed, "Take a good look at this door to look for pressure points." Four of us new students gathered around this door and watched the instructor mark the pressure points.

He stated, "These pressure points are what hold the dents in." He brought over one of the hydraulic tools called a porter power.

He said, "I will show you guys how to get most of these dents pulled out." He clamped the ends of the tool to the edges of the door. He slowly pumped the tool which allowed the hydraulic oil to flow to apply pressure at certain points. By applying outward pressure he was able to slowly pull the door edges outward. He continued this maneuver until the dents started popping out. The banged up door began to start taking its original shape.

I thought to myself, this is going to be fun, especially when we all learn how to use the specialty power tools. Right after the instructor showed us a couple of tricks with the use of a specialty power tool he banged up the door again. When he got done, banging it up for the second time he said, "There, it's all yours – now fix it."

I took a look at the door on both sides to check the damage. I asked the instructor if it would be okay to use the porter power. He let me set it up and checked it before I started pumping the handle. He declared, "Be careful with these power tools."

I replied, "Okay," feeling a little anxious. I managed to get most of the dents out except where there were some nasty creases. I stood there wondering how I would be able to get to the creases. Just then I noticed the instructor helping another student with his door. He was showing him where cuts had to be made to take off the inner portion of the door.

He coached, "This is the easiest way to get to the nasty little creases."

After watching him, I managed to get the inner panel off my door. Again, I stood there wondering how to work on the creases. This time it would take some hand tool to slowly tap the creases into shape. I learned that I had to hold a tool called a dolly under the crease and slowly tap the top with a flat-headed hammer. Now the sheet metal portion was almost reshaped to its original form. Then it was time to slowly grind off the old paint without grinding through the metal. I still ground through the thin metal even after being extra careful. There were small dents that I could see when I looked closely. I noticed more dents by carefully running my hands over the metal. To cover the small remaining dents I used some body filler. After applying it I let the body filler set, and then carefully sanded the body filler into shape. With the outside door panel complete I had to tack weld the inner portion back in place.

To make the welds not so visible I did some careful grinding. I managed to get this much done in repairing the door. One day the instructor looked at my door and asked, "What are you going to do next?"

I replied, "I am going to spray the bare metal with primer before I leave."

"Good; and what will that do?" he asked.

I said, "This will prevent rust from setting in on the bare metal." I did not realize how much time it would take to repair only a door.

When the new students finished repairing our doors, we were introduced to a quicker method. One day we gathered around an advanced student, Dennis, to watch him work. Instead of worrying about the dents he took the outer door panel completely off then put it in the trash. He replaced it with a new panel while he kept the door attached to the vehicle. First he took off the inner panel that was held in place by some simple clips. With the inner panel off he made some simple cuts and the outer panel dropped. He got the new panel and clamped it into place on the door. After doing this he did some simple tack welds to fasten the panel. The panel was new so it required very little sanding.

He sprayed the panel with primer, then sanded it a little again. He confidently stated, "Now the door is ready for a spot paint job." The instructor told us if we wanted to make money, working on commission was the way to go. This meant that the more work was done, the more money was being exchanged between the customers and the body shop. This meant more pay for the auto body repairmen with high commissions.

As my training went on I worked on more vehicles. Each vehicle I worked on was a complete body repair and paint job. In one case I had to replace a cab on a pickup truck. I also replaced several windshields on the vehicles I worked on.

One day I watched the instructor working on the frame machine. Here, he chained down certain portions of the truck frame to connectors on the frame machine. Using hydraulic power he slowly pulled the frame back into its original shape. I learned several tricks from my instructor on how to do the job in less time. I enjoyed the painting portion so I thought some day I wanted to specialize in painting.

I did not complete my training but felt that I learned enough to work as an auto body repairmen. I returned to reality after going on a mental trip back to my past. After speaking with the counselor, Mr. Adams, about attending college, all day long I kept thinking, this sounds like a tough journey.

Chapter Six
Loss of Eyesight

At 22, once again I started having vision problems in my left eye. It was a regular workweek for me but ended in tragedy when this happened. I was doing some building construction near home and did not have to travel too far to work. I was unable to drive a vehicle any longer or read printed material. I tried to focus my vision but it was useless and the view was very lopsided and ugly. I went to the local hospital to have it double-checked. It was the same story as before. I told Dr. Mitchell that I did not want any form of surgery because it would be useless. According to the eye specialist this was a permanent condition. I was going to slowly become blind. I felt that same bolt of fear rush through my body again but this time it was more painful. My eyes watered with tears but I managed to keep from crying. What vision I had at the time slowly faded out and I did completely lose my vision and became totally blind. Just the thought of being blind for the rest of my life was frightening. My stomach turned and my heart seemed to be racing all the time. I felt completely helpless. I would find myself shaking with fear because I did not know what was around me.

I found myself in a world of total darkness every day, not knowing what to expect. Most of the time I just sat in one place at home. I did not want to walk or move around because I was afraid of bumping into something or tripping. I wondered over and over what I did for this to happen to me. I kept asking myself *Why me?* and "It should have happened to someone else." I thought, "There are people out there who probably deserve this more than I do."

I was on an emotional roller coaster, being sad one day and being angry the next. Unable to do the things I enjoyed, I started feeling lonely and left out. My spiritual strength slowly became weaker. It seemed like the important things in life did not matter anymore. I drifted away from family and friends. I started to isolate myself from all activities. I thought this would help ease the pain I was feeling.

Day after day I hoped to see again like I did before but each new day was still dark. Each time I thought of being a blind person I felt a sense of shame and resentment. It was hard to try and do anything because I was afraid of hurting myself. I did not know how to start approaching this devastating way of life. My family did not have any idea how to approach it, either. When it was bedtime I was unable to sleep as I would be restless. I felt there was no hope so I gave up. I stayed home every day even when I was invited to go along. Each day passed by and I became more and more bitter within myself. I did not want to be bothered by anyone. I slowly lost my appetite so as time went on I ate less. I started losing weight and got thin from being of medium build. I felt cheated out of living a happy life. At this point my life had been shattered with no opportunity to rebound. I remember I hardly shed any tears because by this time I thought, "What's the use in crying? It won't change anything."

Being a Native American I sought native healing and had numerous traditional ceremonies performed for me. I was really hoping that the Native American medicine would help me. I gave up this approach after several ceremonies. My family and relatives tried their best to help me but it seemed like we all got exhausted. I thanked my family and relatives for their help and told them it was a very difficult task and journey. By this time I started to lose all aspects of family ties, including the important elements like culture, tradition, values, customs, beliefs, and virtues that were taught to me.

I used to drink beer and whiskey with friends or alone before I became blind. After I became blind I started drinking again. This time, it was more often which became too frequent.

I had my friends or cousin Jayson take me to get beer and whiskey from about 45 miles away from where I stayed. I made sure I had enough booze to last me for a few days. Drinking temporarily put me somewhat at ease. In due time, I went into town to drink at the bars until closing time with a friend or cousin.

By this time, nothing mattered as long as I kept myself intoxicated. I was trying to ease or hide the pain. Whoever I was with, sometimes we did not make it home.

We would spent the night in the truck along the road somewhere. Many times we ended up hitchhiking home in snowy or rainy conditions. I remember my younger brother Stewart and I walked home on the dirt road with mud and rain water everywhere. I drank almost every day and there are times I didn't remember what I did. Somehow throughout all this craziness I made it home or ended up in jail or some safe place.

Many times I woke up, still sad and lonely after a night of drinking with friends. One morning I suddenly woke up alone after a drinking episode. I remember that I was with some friends the night before. I found myself shaking, starting to feel the effects of a hangover. I desperately searched around the house for another drink but could not find any. I kept thinking that my friends never left me without a drink to help ease the hangovers. Just then I heard a vehicle pull up in front of the house where I was staying. Feeling a sense of relief, I was hoping it was my friends who were with me the night before. After the motor went off I heard the car door open and someone getting out. I heard that individual's footsteps approaching the door just as I opened the door and said my greetings in Navajo.

It was my older brother Jerry. He asked, "How are you doing?"

I replied, "I feel bad because of drinking with some guys last night."

"I came by earlier but left because you were asleep." After this I did not say anything – just sat on the couch with my head down.

He spoke again, "I want to ask you something about staying here."

"What is it you would like to say?"

"I would like to know if you want to come and stay with us in Crownpoint." Being there alone most of the time, I thought about giving it a try. I replied, "I'll give it a try and see how it goes."

"Over there you can take a shower and have hot meals to eat."

"Yeah," I replied with a shaky voice.

He concluded, "You can stay with the kids if you want."

Jerry Silago Family Portriat 1985 *(Clockwise Standing Jerry, Shawmarie, Bessie, Seated Eugene, Yvonne, Jerrilene)*

I agreed to go and live at my brother's place with his family for a while. During the weekends, sometimes I went back to Dad's house to spend some time with him. Eventually, I started to get myself back together and put off the drinking. I looked after my brother's children while he and his wife worked during the week.

I managed to do the important things for the kids like giving baths, feeding, dressing, changing diapers and playing games. By being here and doing all these things I felt a sense of being needed which was probably helping me. The children did not really understand my blindness at first. As time went on they started to become aware. As a result of staying with my nieces Shawmarie, Jerrileen, Yvonne and nephew Eugene we became very close. Together we probably watched all the children's television shows that were on at the time. I taught them how to clean or straighten up the house by helping me.

I can recall one time after sweeping the floor, I was going to put the rugs back down. I couldn't find one where I left it. I got on my knees and started to search with my hands. Just then my little niece Jerrileen said, "It's right here." I reached toward her as she pulled the rug away. She said, "Here it is" and tossed the rug at me.

I started laughing, then placed the rug where it belonged. My nephew Eugene and I did a lot of things together as he was growing up. Sometimes I changed the spark plugs on my brother's pickup truck.

I would let him sit under the hood near the plugs. After loosening them I let him unscrew them one at a time. One time I couldn't find him when I was working on something on the truck. I called out his name and he answered me. I said, "Where are you?"

He replied, "Over here under the truck fixing something."

I asked, "Can you come over here first?" He came out and when I touched him he was holding two wrenches. Another time he came inside after playing outside and came up to me. He said, "I am building you a house next to our house."

"A house for me?" I asked.

"Yes," he explained, with new carpet on the floor. I don't know how old he was at the time but I know he was not old enough to start school yet. Another time my older brother Jerry and I were repairing a small dent in one of our younger brother Steve's truck. My niece Yvonne was playing nearby and somehow she got some of the body filler into her hair. My nieces and nephew always brought me happiness, especially when I was feeling down. Over the years the bond between my nieces and nephew and me became very secure. Today we continue to be there for one another.

In the mid 1970s society came out with a gadget called citizens band radio, or CB. Talking on the CB radio was a good pastime for me. My brother Jerry and other friends had CB radios in their pickup trucks so I use to mess around with it.

I got pretty good talking on the CB radio after memorizing the codes. I would be sitting in my brother's truck listening and talking on the CB radio into the late night hours.

There was not too much for me to do as a blind person so the CB radio sort of kept me company. I got to meet several people over the airways. I got to meet some of them in person and we became friends.

Christmas morning this same year I got a large Christmas gift that my brother Jerry and the others were anxious for me to open. I got the gift and started to open it and paused, wondering what it could be as it was rather heavy. Much to my surprise the gift turned out to be a home base CB radio set. The gift was sent to me from my older brother and his family. It was a complete set which included a forty-foot antenna. He said, "One evening you came into my bedroom to ask me something." During this time I guess he was putting the antenna's top portion together. I probably almost messed up the surprise that was being put together for me. The next day my brothers Jerry and Steve and my cousin Jayson assembled the forty-foot antenna and set it up. All the connections were fastened and it was time to try it out. My brothers and cousin drove out of town. As they were getting further away we kept talking with clear reception.

My CB radio came in handy, especially during the winter. I exchanged information with several users about the road conditions. My CB radio could transmit or receive messages from a long range. As time went on there were other home base units set up through out the area. With these other units, transmitting and relaying messages became easier and quicker.

During this CB era I got reacquainted with some of my childhood friends through the airways. After this we spent a good amount of time talking on the CB radio. I also made new friends and some of them came by to visit me and check out my CB radio. One time I was not at home and when we were returning there. We heard my little nieces and nephew talking on the radio. Somewhere along the line the CB radio started to phase out.

While staying at my brother Jerry's place with the children, a Mr. Adams came to see me from Services for the Blind. He came over to talk with me about rehabilitation for blind people. I refused to talk with him so he just left. They sent me information about the program but I did not pay attention to it. Another individual, Mr. Benson, came by again from the same place a couple years later for the same reason. I still did not want to talk with him so again I refused.

Several years into my blindness I continued to stay at my older brother's place off and on. I also stayed with other family members but always returned to Crownpoint. My nieces and nephew were in school and the younger ones were close to starting. Around the same time I lost my dad, which put me into another depression. I went to the Indian Health Service hospital and stayed to deal with this depression. Louise, a nurse at the hospital, told me about a place in Albuquerque where blind people worked. I kind of got curious about this place. Based on the nurse's information, I thought about checking it out. I decided to finally meet with some one from Services for the Blind. The nurse helped arrange for them to come see me at the hospital. During our meeting I asked the counselor, Mr. Adams, if he knew about a place in Albuquerque where blind people worked. He confirmed, "Yes, there is such a place."

I said, "I would like to go over there and try it out."

He replied, "Okay but you have to attend an

131

independent living skills training first." I asked, "Independent living skills training? Where?" He replied, "The training center is located down south in Alamogordo."

"How far away is that?"

"It's about a four or five hour drive from where you live."

"Can I just go to Albuquerque and start working?"

"That would be nice but you need to learn several things first." As our meeting continued he gave me a complete clarification about the orientation center. The information sounded like I would be going back to school. When the gentleman from the Services for the Blind left the hospital I started thinking seriously about school.

Chapter Seven
Orientation Center

After putting off my chances of rehabilitation with the Services for the Blind for several years, I finally allowed myself to at least try the program. I talked again with Mr. Adams, the counselor representing the program. During our conversation, I told him that I wanted to go to work in Albuquerque where blind people worked. He reminded me that I needed to go to the Alamogordo orientation center before anything else. I made a decision to go there to find out what the orientation center had to offer. After my nieces and nephew started school and the loss of my father, I felt that I might try some form of rehabilitation for myself.

One day my brother Jerry, his wife, my nephew Eugene, and Rosie, a close female friend, took me to the orientation center. We drove for several hours to get there. I arrived there not knowing what to expect and feeling a sense of fear.

The staff at the center appeared friendly and fed all of us. They gave us a quick tour of the residential section. They could not show us the training center because we got there on a weekend. My brother's family and my friend had to leave for home because they were working the next day. I had to stay behind at this unfamiliar place. I felt loneliness start to set in along with fear, as this was the first time I had been far away from home as a blind person. I remember that my nephew was very upset because I was staying there and he and his parents had to go home. I missed my nephew and my friend dearly after I heard my brother's truck leave from the front of the orientation center.

I sat in the guest room with teardrops forming as a staff person named Margaret tried to comfort me. I asked her if she could help me get to my room.

She responded, "Yes, take hold of my arm just above my elbow." I took hold of her arm and followed her. We got to my room and after she described the layout she left.

The room had a bed, dresser drawer, closet space and a small sink in one corner. I stayed in there until someone came for me when it was time to eat dinner. Most of the people staying there were back at the center so I got to meet some of them. I did not sleep well that night, as I thought of my nieces, nephew and others at home. I got up early the next morning, took a shower and got ready for the day. Someone came for me to help me to the dining room for breakfast. After breakfast, someone helped me get to the orientation training center.

I came to the orientation center hoping to learn some independent living skills, utilized by individuals who are blind. I met all the instructors who were going to provide the training while I was here.

Much to my surprise, some of the instructors were individuals who also had some level of visual impairment. I found out that there are different levels of blindness. All this time, I had thought being blind meant living in total darkness, like I was.

I started with personal management, cooking, Braille and physical education classes during the morning hours. I took a break to have lunch with the other clients who were also staying there. In the afternoon hours, I took communications skills, mobility cane travel and craft classes. Classes went from Monday through Friday and sometimes on different days we had field trips.

The weekends were hard at first because I did not know anyone there. I stayed in my room most of the time, listening to the radio or a story on a talking book machine. This machine was new to me but I soon learned how to operate it. I could not wait for Monday to come and did not look forward to the weekends like I used to when I had my vision.

In my personal management class I was first introduced to a Braille watch and learned how to tell time using it. Unknowingly I gained some independence by telling time as a blind person. There was also a talking watch and a talking alarm clock. I liked the Braille and talking watch which helped me to tell time for myself. I could not wait to show it to my nieces and nephew back home.

In this same class I learned that plastic Braille tags were available to mark my clothes to identify color. Eventually, I developed my own method by sewing Braille alphabet letters on my shirt tags to help me identify what color I wanted to wear. I never knew there was a special needle so blind people could do their own sewing.

All this time, I'd had someone thread the needle for me so I could sew what I needed to sew. Gaining knowledge about this unique needle also provided more independence.

The instructor, Bess, had a box of play money in dollar bills and coins to help the clients learn how to count their money. I learn a method of identifying bills by folding them in certain ways.

Although I tried using this method I never got used to it. The way I did it was by asking some one I trusted to help me count the bills and place them in order in my wallet by their value. When I went to the store I would ask the cashier for assistance.

I already knew how to identify coins by feeling the edges or their different sizes. There was also a check writing guide available for blind people for those who chose to have a checking account.

When it came to folding different household items I did not have any problems. I already knew how to fold bed sheets, bedspreads, blankets, bath towels and my clothes. I already knew how to wash and iron my clothes. At this center I later realized that most everything would be marked with Braille abbreviated letters. The washing machine, dryer, Coke machine, cook stove and different rooms were marked with Braille. Another method used to help identify or make a selection on a gadget was the use of high marks. I liked this method so today I use the high marks on my washer and dryer, gas stove, and thermostat for my heater, the microwave and my computer keyboard.

There were games designed so blind people could play the same games most people played and enjoyed. The games included Braille deck of cards, checkers, Braille and high marked bingo cards, dominoes, and other games. I learned how to play these games using my sense of touch instead of my vision. I enjoyed playing checkers which I was good at when I had my vision. I never played dominoes as a sighted person, but enjoyed playing them as a blind person once I learned how.

In my cooking class, I learned how to prepare various types of meals. At first the instructor would read what was in the recipe so I could put the ingredients together and cook them. I learned how to prepare lasagna, pizza, burritos, jalapeno cornbread, different cakes and different pies. I already knew how to cook other meals as I cooked for my nieces, nephew and myself. I remember my instructor, Tina, kept asking me to make some Indian fry bread.

I kept telling her I would make some later on. I don't think I made any fry bread but one of the other clients made some. Here again, most everything was marked in Braille and the recipes were in Braille as well. With the skills I already knew, what I learned there made me a better cook. Some staff members liked what the students cooked so they would come into the cooking class to have a snack. I would always tell one of my instructors what I made, and that if he hurried up there, he could have some.

In my Braille class, I got a huge surprise, because I had it all wrong to begin with. I thought Braille was reading raised alphabet letters with your finger tips. When the instructor David told me he was showing me the letter A. I could not believe it because it was a tiny little bump. I always say that I had the best Braille instructor that any one could have. We started with the first five letters in the alphabet during my first week of class.

We worked our way through the alphabet and then moved on to spelling words. I learned how to write and read Braille at the same rate. Eventually I advanced enough to be able to write and read at the grade two level. My instructor was also a totally blind person, just like me. I tried to explain to him what colors looked like, as I'd had my vision before and he had not.

In my physical education class I worked on regaining my physical strength. I started with different floor exercises and stretches. I used a manual treadmill and a stationary cycle for a few minutes a day. I slowly increased the time on the treadmill and the bicycle. I also used the weightlifting machine to work different muscles on my body. Later on I went with the class when they went over to an outdoor oval track to walk. I started walking on this unique track holding on to someone. The track itself was one eighth of a mile long.

What was unique about this track was that there was an aluminum hand rail on the inside curb all the way around the track. After learning the track, the rail helped keep me oriented while I was walking on the track. I slowly built myself up to walking faster, then at a slow jog, then on to running. I remember that I felt great after running alone again for the first time by keeping in contact with the aluminum rail. Eventually I got myself back into running and each time I ran a little farther. I learned how to use the rail and learned how to run with a sighted guide. I gained enough confidence in myself that I entered a five-K race put on by the local crime stoppers. I did well, as I finished second place in the handicapped division and earned myself a medal. When I was home, I continued to run with my nephew Eugene or my younger brother Steve when I was home.

I also learned how to play a game called goal ball which is similar to dodge ball. In it, you don't hit the person; instead you try to get the ball past your opponent. The ball is a little larger then a soccer ball with holes in it and bells inside the ball. By listening, I was able to get a good sense of where the ball was rolling, so I could respond to it. Playing this sport, I was able to further tune my listening skills. I played against two guys, Bill and Tom, all by myself. These guys had been playing this sport for years. After a long game I managed to beat them.

I felt extra special after beating these guys. I also learned how to play a game called beep ball which is similar to baseball. Here we used a regular baseball bat and a regular sized softball with a beeper inside the ball. There were only three bases which were home base, first base and third base. The first and third bases were equipped with a buzzer that could be turned on by a switch.

The pitcher and catcher were individuals with vision because they watched where the ball was at all times. The trick here was to listen for the beeping from the ball and be ready to swing when it comes near, to hit the ball. Each player was allowed to have five strikes instead of the regular three strikes. To score a run when some one hit the ball was to run to whichever base buzzer was turned on. If the player got to the base before any one got the ball it was scored as a run. If the opponent got the ball first it was considered an out. The opponent must verbally indicate that he had the ball to count an out. I could hear the ball whizzing through the air or dashing across the field. Here again, I was fine tuning my hearing that I greatly depended on later in life.

In my communications class, I learned how to type with an electric typewriter. I never did learn how to type as a sighted person. I first learned the different parts of the typewriter. I went on to learn the different keys and their functions. The instructor, Mary, had me listen to cassette tapes using headphones with different lessons recorded on them. This method helped me because I could rewind the tape if I needed to. Eventually, I learned how to type well. I decided to type a letter home to my nieces and nephew to surprise them.

I also found out about different gadgets with an electronic voice, like calculators and adding machines. Here again, I realized that Braille reading and writing were essential to help in the training process.

In my mobility cane travel I learned how to use a white cane and a sighted guide. I learned how to get around indoors as well as outdoors. On my first day of mobility training I was introduced to a white cane made out of fiberglass and very light in weight. I was also introduced to what is called a sighted guide. I would hold on to one of Tommy, the instructor's, arms and just follow him around wherever he went.

He would tell me what was ahead of us, such as doorways, steps, curbs, staircases and others objects. Telling me what was ahead of us helped me to maneuver more efficiently.

First, I learned how to get around indoors using a sighted guide. Next, I learned how to use the white cane for indoor cane travel. Continuing on, I learned how to get around outdoors with a sighted guide. Later on, I started to learn how to do outdoor cane travel. First, I would go for a few blocks with the instructor close to me, giving out instructions. This went on for a while and each day we extended the number of city blocks traveled. Then one day he said, "Okay, buddy, today is your big day. I will follow you or else meet you at 10th street."

I replied, "Okay" as I felt confident and proud of myself. Back home, before coming here, I learned how to get around by listening for different sounds. Remembering how things were when I had my sight was helpful. The white cane and proper use of a sighted guide increased my mobility and confidence. It was not always a perfect walk down the street everyday. I had my share of bumping into signs, street light poles, Coke machines, open doors, chairs, desks and parked vehicles along the curb. I will always have the scars I accumulated over the years. I recall how neat it was to come across another blind person when we meet. Our white canes would tap each other, then at almost the same time we would say our greetings.

In my arts and craft class, I learned to make different projects as a blind person by feel. I made an open faced wall clock that operated by batteries. I also made a cutting board out of wood. I gave the clock and cutting board to two of my brothers. I was able to regain my craftsmanship working with leather. I was able to make belts, wallets, coin purses and other items again. I purchased certain stamping tools and did my own stamping and laced the wallets together myself. This was good as it provided spending money for me when someone wanted a wallet or a belt. I also helped other clients who wanted to learn how to make a wallet or belt for themselves. I made something special for family members and close friends, which I gave as gifts.

One day while sitting around in the lobby of the training center with other clients swapping stories, I received a call from my rehabilitation counselor, Mr. Adams. He said, "Hey partner, I have some good news for you so I made this call."

I responded, "What do you mean some good news? Let's hear it, sir."

He replied, "After reviewing the assessments we did, they show that you have the capability to start a college career."

I said, "A college career, huh? That sounds scary."

He said, "Yes, partner, and if you agree, I will start the process right away."

I replied, "Yes, sir, that will be fine; I will give it a try." After hanging up the phone my mind drifted back to when I attended vocational training after high school. I wondered if this adventure would be similar.

Chapter Eight
Beginning College

After completing several weeks of independent living skills training I took my counselor's suggestion about starting a college career. I went to New Mexico State University's Alamogordo campus with one of the staff from the center. We went there to gather information about the place. I went ahead and applied for admission and financial aid. After being assigned an academic advisor, I registered to take two classes. The two recommended classes I took were introductory classes in psychology and sociology. I met with the sociology professor, Mrs. Jennings, to start getting acquainted with this new journey. During our meeting I stated, "This is the first time I will be attending college and have no idea on where to start."

She replied, "Don't worry; we will make the adjustments as we go along."

I said, "Okay."

"We will find a way to get the books and other class

material read," she reassured me. I got my textbooks and they were pretty thick. I wondered to myself, how the heck, am I going to read these books?

I started attending classes and learned I was the only blind student and the only Native American at this branch campus. I felt very uneasy as I was trying to concentrate on the class lectures. I felt that the other students were always watching me to see what I was doing. I attended classes two days a week, taking each class at different times. I got a girl named Valerie from class to work with as she did the reading.

I was still waiting to get my tape recorder so in the meantime I listened to her read. I finally got my tape recorder which was a fancy gadget with extra features. I started recording the chapters from the textbook as the reader read them orally.

I also started recording the class lectures. I listened to the tapes at the center during the evening and had difficulty in comprehending the material. My reader worked extra hard to help with these two classes.

I had to learn how to get around this small campus with my mobility instructor, Mr. Little. He gave me a complete description of the campus where I would be having my classes. Using what I heard from his description, I placed that imagery in my mind. From this day on, I knew how important it would be to rely on my hearing and memory to continue to guide me. In time, I learned how to find my way around campus. There was always a student wanting to lend a helping hand. One time, a student named Vera asked me, "How should someone approach you if they want to help you?" I told her that all they needed to do was ask if I need help.

As the semester moved on the professors had reviewed at least five chapters in their class. It was time to take my first college exams ever. I kept feeling nervous and restless thinking, what if I failed them? I took each exam orally as each professor read the exam. In one class the questions seemed to be extra long. When the professor finished reading the possible multiple choice answers I had forgotten what the question was asking. This was something new for me and it became frustrating. The professor probably noticed me struggling so she kept encouraging me to try my best. I worked closely with both professors and my reader. I tried to listen to the tapes of the readings and class lectures as much as I could. I didn't know if I was doing the studying correctly. I wondered if there was really a way for a blind student to study; I hadn't the slightest idea.

I went to class each time the class met to try and keep up with the rest. I continued to take my exams, but kept missing a passing score by a point or two.

I kept thinking to myself that I must be crazy, trying to go to college as a blind person. I almost gave up several times, but each time, a student or one of my professors, would hook me and reel me back in. I managed to complete the semester, finding out that psychology and sociology meant studying people individually or as a group.

The semester was finally over and I did not bother to find out how I did for each course. At this point, I probably had my mind made up not to mess with college. I had completed six months of independent living skills training at the center. I made a decision to leave and go home. I returned to Crownpoint and stayed at my younger brother Steve's place for a while. I also stayed at my older brother's Jerry's place with my nieces and nephew. Other times I stayed at my dad's place on the reservation. One day, I received mail from the Alamogordo branch college. I opened it and had someone read it to me. It turned out to be my grades for the two courses I took the previous semester. My nephew Eugene told me I got a D in each class. All this time I was thinking I would receive an F for my grade.

The grades gave my confidence a lift. I kept thinking I already came home and left the orientation center without completing the program. I thought by doing this, I might have jeopardized my chances of further rehabilitation.

I finally got enough courage and contacted my counselor, Mr. Adams, at Services for the Blind. I told him about the grades and asked him if I could have another chance and try the classes again. I told him this time I wanted to try it for me, and not for someone else.

He confidently stated, "Yes it will be okay for you to return to the orientation center to continue training."

I asked, "What about attending classes?"

He replied, "You can continue with classes and we will help you get started."

I did some research about how blind people functioned when it came to attending college. I was introduced to an organization that had textbooks recorded on tape that I could utilize. This was similar to a library and for starters I needed to join the organization. This would allow me to call in and borrow specific textbooks required by each class I would take. With this new resource, I felt a little more confident about getting my textbook read in time and not worrying about getting a reader. I also found out that I could get additional assistance from the student service center at any branch or main campus.

Six months later I returned to Alamogordo to give it another try. I went over to the branch college and signed up for one class during the summer session. I quickly ordered my recorded textbook and picked up a syllabus from the professor. I received the recorded textbook version right away and had a reader, Barbara, from class, read the syllabus onto tape for me. At the beginning of class, I asked my fellow students for their help when they had the time, because I wanted to make it this time around. Without hesitation, I started meeting with a couple of students, Helen and Nancy. The two students alternated their time to work with me. It was sort of difficult at first until I learned how to manage my study time.

I worked hard and managed to receive a passing grade of a C. I felt that this was my C and no one was going to take it away from me.

For the fall semester I established enough confidence to sign up for two classes. These were required ones for an Associate of Arts degree in Psychology. By this time, I had made up my mind to get a degree in Psychology. I wanted to become a counselor, to help other individuals living with a disability. I worked my way up to taking three classes during a regular semester.

With more confidence, I was able to sign up and complete four classes successfully in one semester. Each semester my GPA climbed slowly upward. I can honestly say that I had to work twice as hard as the rest of the students. I worked with good students who took the time and displayed their patience. I also received help from the staff from the orientation center and people I made friends with who were not attending classes.

While at the branch I wanted to sign up for a drawing class. I met with the professor, Mrs. Allison, to figure out a way to do my drawings. She had me practice using clear newspaper print paper, crayons and a window screen. She taped a regular window screen to the table then taped the newsprint over the screen. I used regular crayons to draw, so when I made a mark I could feel with my fingers as the crayon left a mark. She started giving me different objects to draw. I did this by first touching the object and getting a good sense of what the object might look like. I was able to draw different objects and different kinds of animals. I started to create my own pictures in my mind, as I used to draw pictures when I was sighted. My favorite drawing was mountain scenery with rock cliffs, tall trees, a river, a lake or railroad track in the center.

The other favorite of mine was to draw a rodeo scene. I thought to myself I was drawing my younger brother, Jake Jr., in action, riding a bull at a rodeo. The students in my class were amazed at how I was able to create clear pictures. Several of them asked me if they could try drawing something on my screen with their eyes closed. Most of them who tried experienced the difficulty involved. One of my friends, Ronald, made a special board covered with a window screen for me. I used this board to practice and draw pictures away from class. As I spent more time on my drawings they appeared more clear and clean.

As time went on I took a couple more drawing classes. At the end of my last drawing class the professor and students put on their annual art show for the community. I went up to the art show with my good friend Elaine to check it out. When we got there we found out that several of my drawings were on display. They were placed on the wall for the visitors to see. My friend notice a sign placed by my drawings which read "These drawings were done by a totally blind student." I felt very proud, especially when my professor told the visitors that I was the one who did the drawings.

I was still living at the orientation center while attending classes until I was told to move out. I got myself in trouble by violating the center's no alcohol policy. At first it was difficult to try and find a place to live. Being in this situation I almost gave it all up again to just quit and go home. A couple of my close friends, Elaine and April, helped me find a small studio apartment that needed some minor repairs. We made an agreement with the owner about doing the repairs in exchange for rent. I moved into the studio apartment behind my landlord's house and lived there for several months. Living there I had to learn how to get around using my white cane. I later moved into a single bedroom apartment toward the center of town. The independent living skills I already knew and the ones I learned from the center helped me live independently. Just like anyone else I paid rent, paid utilities, and bought food, housekeeping needs and personal items. I was living on a fixed income, so I applied for the state's food stamp program.

I was eligible to receive the stamps, which helped me

buy food. I enjoyed living in my one bedroom apartment. My two special friends, Elaine and April, were always there to help me. One of them lived in town and the other one lived up in the mountains. I spent a good number of happy moments with these friends. Sometimes I spent time up in the mountains. Other times I spent it with my friend in town.

My brother Jerry and his family came down to visit several times. One time I heard someone knocking on my screen door. The knock sounded like it was coming from little hands.

I asked, "Who is out there?"

I heard a little girl's voice. She said, "It is me." I recognized the voice and it was one of my little nieces, Jerrileen.

I replied, "Who are you with?"

She answered, "With everybody."

I asked, "Where are they?"

She said, "They're still in the truck." I opened the screen door, then lifted her up and hugged her for a while. The rest of the family came in. Later that day my brother and his wife prepared a good traditional meal for me. The next day we all went out sightseeing in the area to the Space Hall of Fame, My niece Shaw really liked one of the rockets named Little Joe and wanted to take it home. My other brothers Steve and Jake Jr. and sisters Etta and Gracie also came by to visit which helped me to stay motivated with my journey. When family members came to visit we treated my friends Elaine and April to hot Indian fry bread which they enjoyed.

The big day came when I completed my course work and received an AA degree in Psychology. Over the duration of this course work I had to overcome many challenges that a blind person encounters to make it in college. I was treated the same way every other student was treated, having to meet each task they did.

I appreciated the help I received from several students who were proud of my accomplishment. With the hard work and determination I came out with a good overall grade point average. This would allow me to pursue a bachelor's degree, if I desired.

Returning to the reservation, I started looking for a job with an AA degree in Psychology. I wanted to work in an environment where I could help people. I felt that with an AA degree, being fluent in Navajo would be a plus. I tried several places, but each attempt led to a dead end. One day my older brother Jerry suggested, "You should go back to school and get a bachelor's degree to help you get a good job."

Astonished, I said, "A bachelors degree?"

He replied, "I have confidence in you that you are capable in getting it." I thought to myself that would be a lot of work as just getting the AA degree took a good amount of work. Some where along the line I made up my mind to check into attending New Mexico State University. I thought that if I waited any longer I might lose my confidence and acquired skills. I traveled to Las Cruces, going through Alamogordo, to check it out with my sister Gracie. We stayed in Alamogordo at my friend Elaine's house. During our stay at my friend's place she stated, "I have all the confidence in the world that you will make it at NMSU." The next morning we went over to Las Cruces to take care of the necessary paperwork.

I was all registered to start classes at NMSU's

main campus for the spring semester. I was on another journey to work towards a bachelor's degree in psychology. I signed up for four classes which was going to be kind of rough at first. I thought to myself that there were probably more resources there to make up the difference.

I previously learned that if I got the necessary information pertaining to textbooks, I could order my books on tape early. I had time that day, so I ordered the textbooks required for each class.

It was time, so with more confidence, I again left Crownpoint for school, catching the bus a couple of days before classes began at the university. I spent that night at my friend Elaine's house in Alamogordo. The next day she took me to Las Cruces to get my room, as I was going to stay in the dormitory. I got to my room and there was another student there named Teddy. I introduced myself and told him that I would be staying there with him for the semester.

"That will not be a problem," he said. I noticed that my section of the room was disorganized. Quickly my friend and I got this section in order. She said, "I hate to do this but I have to be getting home."

I replied, "That's okay, I'll be fine." I asked her before she left if she could show me where the front office for this dorm was. She showed me the simplest route as she was familiar in working with blind individuals.

After she left I walked over to the front desk. I was able to make it over and when I got there the person at the front asked me if I needed any help. I told her that I was starting to learn my way around here. She assured me, "If you need any help come to the front or call the front desk."

I asked, "Okay; can you show me where I will be receiving mail?"

She responded, "Sure, come this way, the mailboxes are right over here." I walked over to where she was talking from. She asked, "What is your room number?"

Room 516."

She explained, "Your mailbox is the same as your room number." Then she showed me where I could find my mailbox. "I think it would be a good idea to show you where the laundry room is now." I agreed and followed her out the door and around the corner. "Here it is. If you need any help, let me or whoever is working know."

I asked, "Okay; how much does it cost to wash and dry?" She told me and I followed her back to the front.

"I can make it back to my room from here."

"Are you sure?"

Just then a student named Luther approached us. He stated, "I can help you to your room."

I replied, "Okay buddy."

He asked, "Are you a new student here?"

"Yes, I'm a junior psychology major."

"You just gave my confidence a boost."

"That is great."

He said, "I want to wish you the best of luck."

The next morning came and I got myself ready for class and stepped out the door. I stood there with my white cane and backpack. I heard some people walking toward me. When these people got close enough I stopped them and asked, "Excuse me, would it be possible for one of you to help me out?"

One of them replied, "Sure; how can I help you?"

I explained, "I need to get to my first class; here is my class schedule."

After taking a look she calmly stated, "Let's go; it's right over there across the street." Then she gently took hold of my arm.

"Good," I said and walked alongside her.

"I have a class in that same building." She told me her name was Mary and I told her mine. She asked, "What is your major?"

"I am majoring in psychology and hope some day to become a counselor."

"That's great."

"I hope to help other people with disabilities and my native people some day."

"If you don't mind can I ask you a different question, about your eyes?"

I responded, "That's fine with me, I will try and answer it for you the best I can."

"Can you see any with your left eye?"

"No but if you close your eyes very tight this will give you an idea what my vision is like."

She compassionately commented, "I have my eyes closed right now, and it is dark so it must be rather difficult."

I replied, "Yes, it gets pretty difficult at times but I manage to maintain my self-confidence." People always ask me this question because my left eye appears like I can see with it. My right eye appears discarded because of the previous eye surgery so I wear sunglasses.

She helped me to the classroom and to reassure me said, "Good luck! You have a lot of courage to do what you are doing."

I sat in the front row so I could get good reception on my tape recorder. The professor, Mrs. Yearly, introduced herself and handed out the syllabus. She went over the syllabus and made sure each student had the correct textbook for class.

Near the conclusion of class she asked if anyone had any questions, so I raised my hand. She gave me the go ahead to ask my question. I introduced myself and asked the students if one of them could help me get over to the American Indian Program office. A girl named Kim volunteered to help me after class. As I met briefly with the professor, she reassured me, "We will make necessary adjustment as the semester progresses." I walked over to the AIP building with Kim, who asked me if I would need any help with our class. I replied, "Yes, that would be great." I told her where I was staying on campus. We reached the office and I stated, "We can meet when we both have time."

"Okay," she agreed.

Before she left she took a look at my class schedule and compared it to hers. She stated, "I think this will work out well for both of us."

I met with Mr. Baker, my counselor at the AIP office who was a Native American from a different tribe. He you doing, and asked, "How are you and how can we help you today?"

I replied, "The first thing I need help with is getting around campus until I learn my way around."

He responded, "No problem" and called over another person, Mr. Jefferson, from a different department. The program he managed assisted disabled students. The gentlemen who came was located in the same building.

He had some level of visual impairment, but could still read and had no problem getting around. Apparently he attended this university and graduated.

I told him the dorm where I was staying and showed him my class schedule.

"I will start coming over about 20 minutes before your class starts and get you situated."

I replied, "Okay."

"When you are not in class, I want to start getting you familiar with other places on campus."

"Yes, especially the cafeteria," I said.

He suggested, "After we are done here, let's walk over to your dorm and start working on you making it to the cafeteria."

"Okay."

The other counselor asked, "What else do you need besides getting around campus?"

I replied instantly, "For starters, I need at least one reader to help me by reading the class syllabus and handouts onto tape for me."

"I will get a student from our work study program as soon as I can."

"I already have my textbooks on tape so I can start reading."

"Let me take a look at your syllabus," he requested.

I said, "Okay" and handed it to him.

"You need to read chapter one before your next class."

"Good; now I will start getting busy."

"In case we don't get a reader right away, bring your syllabus from each class so we will make sure you have them on tape."

"Okay I have a tape recorder and some blank tapes for recording."

"If you need anything please don't hesitate to inform me."

"Okay," I replied, smiling at him.

"Before you leave I want to introduce you to the rest of the staff." I met the other staff and a couple of work-study students. The services I would receive from these two programs gave me a confidence boost.

Compared to the branch college in Alamogordo, this was a large campus with sidewalks going in every direction. I left the AIP office with the gentleman from the disability services department. Right away he started to describe the layout of the sidewalk from the office to my dorm. I got a good diagram of his description in my mind right away.

The sidewalks were something like highways with intersections. He said, "Some of the sidewalks are wider than the others, with curves." We started from my dorm room and worked our way to the cafeteria and into the building. We reversed ourselves and worked our way back to my dorm room. We walked this route several times until I was able to learn the shortest and simplest way. The cafeteria employees were another group of awesome people on campus. Each time I entered the cafeteria I got assistance in getting my breakfast or dinner. I made friends with several of the workers at the cafeteria. Somewhere between my dorm room and the cafeteria was the sidewalk that led to the AIP office.

Sometimes on my way to the cafeteria I would stop by the AIP office to say hello to the gang. With the help of the two programs and several students I made it to my classes and other places throughout the semester.

Each semester I had new classes in different buildings. So this meant that each time, I had to learn new routes to get to my classes. I took classes during the regular semesters and summer sessions. Some of my classes were in regular classrooms and others were in a lecture hall. On the first day of one of my psychology classes there were over 200 students – but the enrollment dropped right after the first exam.

I made friends with several students on campus. Some of them volunteered to help me with my homework assignments and with completing my term papers. One classmate, Anna, volunteered her time to provide extra tutoring for a couple of the more difficult courses. As time went on the two of us became close friends. I enjoyed attending school at NMSU and each day was a challenge for me as well as for the professors and students. I had my share of frustration with classes trying to understand what the professor was talking about.

I did a good amount of listening to my textbook tapes and lecture tapes. Sometimes I would fall asleep while listening to a tape. I think this was when I had been listening for hours. I recorded classroom lectures and circulated several cassette tapes for each class. I kept track of the cassette tapes and other items by labeling them with Braille. One day one of my helpers, Kelly, asked me how I kept track of my folders and cassette tapes. I told her that I had them labeled in Braille and showed them to her.

She said, "This is amazing."

"Yes it is, and if you like I can try and teach you some Braille," I replied.

"That would be nice; I bet it is difficult."

"Yes, it is at first, and it takes a lot of patience."

Each time I had a chance I tried walking out there alone and sometimes I got myself disoriented. When I did I would ask someone nearby for help. One day a couple of students came up to me. One of them asked, "Hey, is it okay if I try out your white stick?"

I replied, "What do you mean, 'try out my white stick'?"

"What I mean is I want to see how it feels to be blind."

I replied, "Oh, okay, but you have to keep your eyes shut all the time and this will not give you the feel you are looking for."

The other student intervened, saying, "I'll watch him closely because I don't trust him."

"Okay, here you are, tough guy." He tried it out and quickly stopped.

He replied anxiously, "I don't think I could survive as a blind person."

"What about you? Do you want to try it."

She replied, "No, thank you, I am already scared and can't imagine how you do it everyday."

I responded, "I don't have any other choice."

She asked, "What about those dogs that lead blind people around?"

"I never really thought about having a dog because it is a traditional thing." I learned the campus enough to make it to my classes and the cafeteria with more confidence. I would be walking back from the cafeteria or class and one of my readers would catch up with me and say, "You are doing great by learning more about your way around."

I replied, "I owe many thanks to all the people like you who took the time to help me."

"It has been a pleasure helping you – I wish I could do more."

The more knowledgeable I got with the campus layout the more walking I did. I did this to explore new areas as well as for exercise.

Sometimes students would offer their help when they saw me out there. I would tell them that I was out learning more about unfamiliar areas. By this time, between my hearing and memory I was able to get around all over campus. One particular day during one of my summer session classes, it was getting pretty close to time for class to begin so I was trying to walk as fast as I could. I must have been walking pretty fast and passed the sidewalk that led to my classroom. I kept going at a good pace and suddenly tripped over a small wall about two feet high. Apparently the wall surrounded a gold fish pond. When I tripped I fell into the pond holding my cane in one hand and my tape recorder with the other. There were some students who saw me fall into the pond so they came over quickly and pulled me out. I still had my cane in one hand and still held onto my tape recorder. Standing there with water running off my clothes I heard water coming out of my recorder. One of the students, Rudy, nervously asked, "Are you all right?"

"Yes; is my cowboy hat still in the water?"

, "Yes; let me use your stick to get it out."

Another student nearby was trying to get the water out of my tape recorder. I let them help me get back to my dorm room to change my clothes. I was okay after changing my clothes and my hat dried off. I went to see my professor, Mr. Smith, to tell him what happened and to turn in my homework after letting it dry off. Together we had a good laugh about what happened to me earlier. He stated, "You stay away from that fish pond."

As for my tape recorder, I let it dry out completely before trying it out and was able to use it to finish out the summer session. In the meantime I placed an order for a new recorder right away with the help of my brother Jerry. It took about a month for a new recorder to make it to me.

I maintained my serenity by dealing with the loneliness, missing the family and especially the children. Some weekends I went out with friends or traveled to Alamogordo to visit my friend Elaine.

I tried to make sure that I read all my assignments and completed my homework before going anywhere. The two other things I kept up with were cleaning my dorm room and doing my laundry. I had learned to do this when I stayed at the dorm while attending high school. I learned that when I signed up for a new semester I tried to leave Fridays open. This was because I enjoyed going to Alamogordo to visit my friend or cross the border into Mexico. It was nice to have a three day weekend. I remember that by Friday afternoon the campus was deserted and came back to life the following Monday.

I kept in touch with my brother, his family, and other family members by phone. I also went home for quick weekend visits. I made friends with students who were from my home town. These guys would let me know that they were going back to Crownpoint for the weekend and planned to return in time for class on Monday. I went with these guys a couple of times and pitched in for gas. Other times, I would make arrangements to meet one of my brothers somewhere between Las Cruces and home, usually in Albuquerque. Sometimes one of them would bring me back down. It was about a six hour drive each way.

Near completion of my first year of school, I ran into a sticking point. I got myself involved with alcohol use again. I started sliding downwards and began missing classes. Luckily for me it was at the tail end of my semester, so I was able to complete my coursework.

I managed to make good grades and accumulate 36 credit hours toward my bachelor's degree, thanks to my fellow students and family support for not messing up. I left school and went home for the break which was for about a month.

I tried working out my personal problems while at home but kept everything to myself. I enjoyed being home with family and all the home cooked meals.

Once again I returned to school to start my second year. I got myself familiar with my new classrooms and the routes to class. I had learned my way around this campus and the stores near by. I remember one crosswalk where they installed a device with a cuckoo bird sound, alerting one that it was safe to cross at the traffic light. I crossed at this intersection many times, especially on Sunday, to get me a deli sandwich to eat. I made several new friends who always offered their assistance. I taught my friends how to be a sighted guide in case they wanted to help another blind person. Sometimes I would just go walking with a couple of my friends, using them as sighted guides. I started using alcohol again on weekends with these new friends and my drinking started to get out of hand. About four weeks into this semester I was unable to perform school work efficiently. I started missing classes and fell behind with note taking and reading assignments. The residential advisor got in contact with me and warned me about my drinking. I neglected the warning, and kept on drinking until I was told to leave. I left the dorm and thought I would attend classes from a friend's apartment. This was not the case as I was informed that I was suspended from school. I was informed that the only way I could attend again was to complete an inpatient alcohol abuse treatment program.

Right away I admitted myself to an alcohol rehabilitation treatment program away from school. The rehabilitation program helped me to reconnect with the important things in life. I was able to relate to other individuals with the same problem. Through group cohesiveness I unveiled issues that were painful and troublesome at the time.

In reality I probably drank because I wanted to and it was not a forced choice. I successfully completed the program and made new friends as well. I was on my way home to Crownpoint and stopped at the university to check in with the residential advisor. He told me to check in with the business office which did not sound too good. Instead I went straight over to the AIP office and told the director, Mr. Nelson, and the counselor, Mr. Baker, about my situation. They reassured me that I would be back in school for the summer session and not to worry. I gave them a copy of my certificate of treatment completion and other documents before leaving for home. Leaving NMSU I caught the bus to Alamogordo and stayed with my friend Elaine for a couple of days. We talked about what I had gotten myself into again using alcohol. I called home to let them know when I would be arriving in Gallup so someone could meet me there. After all the arrangements were in place I caught the bus again, this time for home. I stayed home for a couple of months thinking about what had happened. I came back to the university before summer sessions began and provided the administration the necessary paperwork for reinstatement. After a lengthy discussion I regained my active student status. I would be allowed to live in the dorm on campus again with restrictions. I thought to myself that I had to be careful because I might not get another chance.

Summer session was near so I was allowed to continue school on campus. Returning, I got right back into the swing of school work. I had friends who were supportive of my sobriety and those who thought it was okay to drink.

I thought to myself that if I wanted to get my degree I had to completely abstain from alcohol use. When some of my friends wanted to go out drinking I refused to go with them. Just like everything else in life there is always going to be some wild and crazy thing popping up. It so happened that a story came out about a drinking episode over the weekend at my dorm. This guy was visually impaired. I was approached to answer some questions because of my living situation. I had to meet with some dorm officials to answer the questions they had. Before anything I went over to the AIP office and told them what happened. The counselor Mr. Baker asked me if I was drinking. I told him I did not and it must have been someone else. When it was time to meet with the dorm staff I went over with the counselor who was very helpful.

I got myself involved with other activities on campus. The university activity center had good things to offer. For example, one weekend my friends Margie and Ken and I rented a couple of canoes. We took the canoes up river and started back down. This was my first time in a canoe floating on top of the river. I felt a bit anxious after visualizing what the river looked like in my mind. I know that these waters are powerful. I felt a little sense of security wearing a life jacket. I was on one canoe with my friend Margie and her son. After cruising down river awhile she said, "Lean over to your left side when I say now."

I replied, "Lean over? Why?"

She warned, "There are some tree branches up ahead hanging over the bank."

I replied, "Okay" and just then she yelled out, "Now lean." We must have leaned too far over at the same time because when we did we continued to roll. The canoe turned over and we were all in the water. I was completely lost and noticed I was going down river quickly. I don't know what was happening but it felt like I was tumbling under water. I honestly felt I was going to drown and die in this river.

All of a sudden, I heard my other friend Ken yelling, "Stand up right there. The water is not very deep." I thought my friend was way off in the distance but he was near me. He said, "Hey, buddy, reach over to your right side and grab hold of the canoe."

"Here it is," I responded with relief, grabbing on and breathing rapidly. I jabbered, "Man, that was real scary and it seemed like it took forever floating around alone."

My friend Margie asked, "Are you okay?"

"Yes, I'll be all right."

"Guess what, we lost our lunch. It all went down river."

I replied, "I guess that means my stuff was also lost."

"Yep, everything we had on the canoe is gone." We managed to regroup and continue down river. It started getting cloudy and my friends said, "It looks like it's going to rain." At that instant I smelled rain off in the distance. They suggested that we should start thinking about getting out of the water. It was a good thing we did because it started to rain with lightning. We took the canoes out and loaded them on my friend's truck. We went back to their place where we ended the day with a barbecue.

I also got myself involved in working out at the weight room. By this time I had learned my way to the activity center and also how to get around inside. I liked doing a light workout with the weight machines. I also enjoyed using the stationary cycle.

One time, I was slowly making my way toward the exit door after a work out. I heard Robert, one of my readers, calling my name. I stopped and said, "Hello, there."

He called, "Come this way toward my voice for a minute." I started walking toward his voice but stopped in my tracks.

He grumbled, "Come on, dude what's going on?"

I replied, "Wait up; I am thinking about something." I started walking again and just then I heard a basketball bouncing where he was. He said, "Over here, dude, – now stand right there."

"Right here?"

"Yes, that will do." I stood there and listened to what was going on just then I heard a familiar girl's voice. I recognized that voice and said, "Hello, Karen, what are you guys up to?"

She answered, "Hi, we want to let you try something if it is okay with you."

"That depends on what it is."

"We would like for you to try and make a free throw from the free throw line."

"Yeah, I can try that," I responded confidently.

The other guy said, "Here is the ball" and then turned me toward the goal. I suggested, "Wait; here, take my cane and tap on the rim so I can have an idea where it is."

They agreed, "Great; that is a good idea." I tried about 15 times and managed to make several after getting my range and rhythm. My friends Robert and Karen were laughing with joy and commented, "Good job." She suggested, "Maybe we can play ball sometime, huh?"

I replied, "Yes; I have a good idea for you guys."

Curious they asked, "What is that idea of yours?"

I muttered, "The both of you can wear blindfolds

when we play." Just then I heard one of them at the free throw line. She said, "I want to try making a basket with my eyes closed."

I said, "Wait up; let us tap the goal so you can hear where it is." Robert started tapping the goal as she threw the ball and missed. She said, "This is rather difficult but interesting, huh?"

I completed the summer session and the next two semesters without drinking. During this time I had a special friend Anna who kept me busy as she tutored and drilled me for each class. This paid off as I made the dean's list by achieving a perfect 4.0 grade point average during one of the remaining semesters. I completed the necessary requirements to receive a bachelor's degree in psychology. My special friend Anna, faithful readers and dedicated tutors were proud of the accomplishment. I told them that by helping me they were a part of this accomplishment. I also told them that they were always there for me and that was what really counted.

During my last semester at NMSU a Navajo gentlemen, Mr. Banally, came to my dorm room. He was referred by the people who worked at the AIP office. He said, "I heard you are graduating at the end of this semester."

I replied, "Yes, with a bachelor's degree in psychology."

He said, "I got good recommendations about you from the people at the AIP office."

"Is that right?" I asked.

"Would you be interested in working for me on the reservation in Arizona?" he asked. A thought crossed my mind that very instant about my wanting to help my Native people on the reservation. I remembered that I wanted to become a counselor to help my people and others needing some help.

"What type of work are you talking about?" I asked.

He said, "Working as a special education teacher at a rehabilitation center."

"A special education teacher?"

"You will be working with young Navajo adults with a disability."

"I can come visit the center after I graduate from here."

"I am interested in hiring a Navajo person who is fluent in the language."

I responded with self-assurance, "I am fluent in our language."

"Good. I will be waiting for your visit."

The big day came when the majority of my family came down to Las Cruces to attend my graduation. Prior to the ceremony the administration asked me about an escort to help me. They offered to provide an escort for me.

"I would like to have my nephew Eugene escort me when I go up to get my diploma," I responded. "It is very important to me because the two of us are very close." I thought besides that I would be an inspiration for my nephew, nieces and others. I practiced with my nephew during the graduation practice exercises. The time came to walk up to the podium to get my diploma. My nephew Eugene and I walked up there with the rest of the graduating class with feelings of a great accomplishment. I probably felt extra proud because I was with my nephew and the rest of the family was in the audience.

The Pan American Center was jam packed with hundreds of people hugging and congratulating their graduates. I remember the majority of my family made the six hour drive to attend my graduation. Most of my readers and friends were also among the crowd. After all the handshakes and hugs I went back to the motel with my family. There, I shared a special cake that my exceptional friend Anna brought for me. This was a different kind of cake as I had never tasted one like this before. I recall my special friend's husband kept wanting to eat some of the cake and I don't know if he ever did. The next day we went over to one of the popular restaurants to have breakfast. I still remember we waited outside with several other people and the establishment were serving pastries, coffee and fruit juices. After breakfast we decided to make one last cruise around the campus as we followed each other.

My nephew Eugene and I rode with my younger sister Cynthia as we led every one. We continued to follow each other as we headed for home. I went back to Crownpoint to stay with my older brother Jerry and his family.

I was thinking about checking out the job offer at the rehabilitation center on the reservation in Arizona. I started to miss NMSU, always wondering what my friends who were still in school were doing. I called the AIP office to let them know what I was up to and each time they asked me to come down for a visit.

Archie at graduation with Suzanne, one of his readers.

Chapter Nine
Back to Work

It was time, so, armed with a bachelor's degree, I went to visit the rehabilitation center in Arizona. I met with the administration staff and the job sounded good. They offered me a teacher's contract position with living quarters. I accepted the offer and submitted all pertinent documents. I had to travel to Phoenix, Arizona to complete the remaining paper work. I thought about my last day of work when I was a sighted person, which was back in December, 1973. When I had my vision I did mostly physical work. Now I would be working with people so I thought, "This is what I wanted to do." I remembered saying at the beginning of my journey, "I want to come back to the reservation to help my people."

I needed to get to Phoenix to meet with the people at the Arizona Department of Education. It was summertime, so I asked my younger brother Steve about making a trip to Phoenix since he was off for the summer.

He said, "Yeah, we can go with another driver." One day my younger brother Steve, nephew Jackson and I took off on this adventure. We arrived at the rehabilitation center to meet with the administrative assistant, Mr. Banally. After our meeting he instructed us, "Follow me over to St. Johns where I will be getting some papers authorized." He left in his truck so we followed him, driving for a couple of hours. We arrived there and he said, "You can wait here; it will not take long for me to get these papers signed." I replied, "Okay," and the three of us waited. Steve and Jackson were looking around and describing what the landscape looked like.

Just then my nephew whispered, "Here comes your buddy." The gentlemen came back and stated, "Here you go, take these papers to Phoenix."

I replied, "Okay, we are on our way."

"Good luck; have a safe trip."

"Okay; is there anything else?" I asked

"When you get all the forms signed, bring them back to me."

I replied, "All right – I will have them back to you as soon as I can."

"Okay; see you then." None one of us had been to Phoenix by the route we were going to take.

As we drove, we my brother and nephew described what the scenery looked like along the way. Three areas I remember well are the Salt River Canyon, a tunnel through the mountains and the giant cactus standing in the flats. We stopped along the edge of the Salt River Canyon where there was space for sightseeing. We also stopped by one of the cactus that was near the road. We went up to the cactus so I could touch it. I was surprised as to how huge and tall they stood. My brother Steve told me that these huge cactus were standing up on both sides of the highway as far as one could see. We continued driving and arrived in Phoenix in the late afternoon hours. We got ourselves a motel room and got something to eat after checking in. My brother and nephew wanted to get some cold beer to drinks so they did. I didn't want to be late for my appointment so I got to bed before they did. In the morning each of us got ready and we went for some coffee and doughnuts for a quick energizer.

Jerry, Jake, Mom, Jackson, Steve, Archie

I met with some people for over an hour at the office where I was supposed to go. Then I waited in the waiting room until they called me again.

I was informed that I was eligible for a certification to

teach at the rehabilitation center. I also had to take two courses and turn in my grades before a year passed.

My nephew Jackson said, "When we walked out, everybody kept staring at us." I teasingly replied, "If they only knew who we really are."

He responded, "Yeah" and laughed. I added,

"They don't even know that my brother is a school teacher in New Mexico."

My brother Steve teasingly responded, "Yeah, that's right – let's get out of here before they find out."

I asked, "Okay, boys, are you ready to eat a real meal, besides coffee and doughnuts?"

Jackson quickly replied, "Yeah, I am starving."

My brother said, "I am hungry, too." We drove around looking for a Mexican restaurant to eat some enchiladas.

We found a place that looked like it would serve a good Mexican meal with hot chili. After our meal we headed out of Phoenix on the freeway that would take us to Flagstaff. I recall while driving downhill that the diesel semi trucks would zip right by us. We caught up with them and passed them back going up hill. The scenery here had mountains and a lot of tall pine trees. We decided to take a detour from the freeway and go around Oak Creek Canyon to check it out. We drove and walked around this beautiful place for a while. Afterwards we headed out for Flagstaff, arriving there later in the afternoon. Since we had the opportunity, the three of us continued our detour by visiting the Grand Canyon. When we got there we went over to the edge and right away I started to back off because I felt very uncomfortable. Later my brother and my nephew talked me into walking with them down a canyon path to a certain point. We were not allowed to pass this point without the proper hiking equipment. They promised me they would take good care of me so I went along.

It was early in the evening and they did an awesome job of describing what the place looked like. There were some pretty colors being displayed by Mother Nature at the time. We headed out of Grand Canyon by night fall and grabbed a hamburger along the way. We drove through the Hopi and Navajo reservations of Arizona most of the night.

We got back to my brother's place early the next morning. We all slept for a while until we got some rest. I ask my brother if he could take me back to Crownpoint. Our nephew was headed back home. The boys said, "We enjoyed the trip; it gave us a chance to get out for a while."

I got back to Jerry's place in Crownpoint to tell him and his family the good news. I told them I would need some help to clean the trailer I was going to live in. I told them this would be in about three weeks which would be a week before work began. We went over there when the day came to clean out the trailer.

My sister-in-law Bess said, "You need some curtains."

"Is that right?"

"I can probably make you some if you get the material."

"Okay," I said and had my nephew Eugene help me measure the windows. They all agreed, "It looks more like a home after we cleaned it." I had to return in a week so we planned to be back with some food and curtains. My younger sister Jolene who lived in the area with her family also helped us with the cleaning. When we were all done we went over to a fast food joint to grab a bite. I told my sister that we would be back next week. She was happy that I was going to work there. After returning to Crownpoint my nephew Eugene and I went into Gallup the next day to check on some furniture. After reaching a reasonable deal, the furniture company agreed to deliver some in about a week.

I was ready so I return to my new home to move in and get ready for my first day of work. The trailer had a refrigerator, a gas range, a dining table and four chairs. We put up the new curtains my sister–in-law Bess made. We also put away the food we bought. In a way it was neat as we were all just laying around on the carpet without any furniture.

I borrowed a mattress from my sister Jolene to sleep on until my furniture was delivered. I slept on the mattress on the living room floor for at least a week. I brought my portable radio so I could have something to listen to. In the mean time, I also ordered telephone service and cable TV. In about a week or so my furniture was delivered which brought the trailer to life. My telephone and cable TV were also connected so I was in business.

With the help of my sister getting me to my first day of work I walked into the classroom. I met Angie and Paula, the two teaching assistants who were going to help me. Together we all walked to the cafeteria in another building. There was a "welcome back to school" event going on. I was introduced by the assistant administrator, Mr. Banally. After being introduced

I heard someone walking toward me. That individual came up to me and said, "My teacher." The students were young adults with developmental disabilities. Thinking about this I felt afraid because I thought he was going to grab me or something like that. I stood there without moving as he approached me and put his arms around me and greeted me in the Navajo language. At this instant the fear left my body and I smiled and greeted him back.

I had to learn quickly how to get back and forth from my trailer to the school building. This was about a 300 yard walk one way. With the help of my sister Jolene during this first week, together we maneuvered around the architectural barriers. I learned how to get around inside the classroom area and the cafeteria.

It did not take very long to learn the school grounds and the trail to my new home. It was all close together and I always got help from the other staff living in the same area. I did get myself disoriented a few times, but that was to be expected.

There were sidewalks on the school grounds but once I left the campus it was all dirt. The maintenance workers here put up a small fence that I followed back to my trailer. The fence ran along side the road that ended close to my new home.

Together with my assistants, Angie and Paula, we worked with each student on a one-to-one basis. We did our teaching using both the Navajo and English languages. We had two groups of students – one for the morning class and the other for the afternoon. My assistants had worked there for several years, so, they provided me with updated information. This made working with the students less difficult.

As time went on I got to know some of the students well. For example, I had one student, Herman, who stopped by my classroom right after breakfast or just before class started. He would tell me about what he dreamed about the night before. Some of the students would talk about their horse or about herding cattle or sheep. Some of the students recognized my blindness, so they helped by leading me. This took place especially when I was leaving to go home. A couple of them would walk me to the outside gate. Sometimes they would wait for me there in the morning and grab on to my arms to lead. I showed them my appreciation which made them feel good. There were times we had some problems with the students' aggressiveness but the majority of them did well.

The holidays during the school year brought excitement for both the students and staff. Prior to a special event, I sent out an invitation to each parent. Most of the time, we got a good response from the parents as they showed support for their child. I talked with some of the parents as they provided additional information. The students went home over the Thanksgiving, Christmas and spring breaks.

When they came back they had a lot to tell me. Sometimes I stayed a few minutes late after school to listen to their stories. I felt this did them good and they had some understanding that I cared about them. Other times I went to the cafeteria to have lunch with them. We also went on field trips and had several cookouts away from the center. I recall one field trip when we went to Gallup to the bowling alley. Afterwards the students and staff members enjoyed lunch at a pizza place. Giving them the time and attention brought about changes in their behavior. Toward the conclusion of the school year I had gotten used to the students as a group and individually. At the end of the school year, I was informed that I did not get my teaching contract renewed. In spite of this I completed the contract with dignity and decided to leave the area. The students would be who I missed the most after leaving because we had an understanding.

After finding another job I started working as a vocational rehabilitation counselor in Gallup. This job involved working with individuals having a physical or mental disability. This job was advertised in the newspaper. So, I contacted the program and found out that the main office was in Albuquerque. The closing date was near so I got my information sent to them quickly. The next step was an interview. I went in for my interview and during this time I was nervous because this was my first government job. The interview went along okay. I met with the area supervisor and a couple of vocational rehabilitation counselors. They told me that there were several individuals who applied and they would get back with me.

I left the office and went home wondering what these people might be thinking about my blindness. I also thought about what level of education the other applicants had.

One day I received a letter from the main office stating that I was scheduled for another interview. Finding this out lifted my self-confidence. I went for my second interview feeling more relaxed. I made sure I got there a little early. The second interview went smoother then the first one did. I left the office feeling more confident than after the first interview. One day I received a phone call and the gentleman identify himself Mr. Long. He said, "I am offering you the counselor's position you interviewed for."

I proudly responded, "I am interested in taking the position."

He indicated, "I need you to report for work on this date."

I was staying at my mother's house during this time. I told her what the phone call was about. She cheerfully stated, "I am glad and happy for you that you got the job."

I explained, "I need to go back to Crownpoint and ask Eugene to help me find a place to live in Gallup." One Saturday morning my nephew and I got an early start after a good breakfast. Plans were to look at several places listed for rent in the newspaper. Later in the afternoon, we found a small house set adjacent to the owner's huge house. I spoke with one of the daughters, Ellen, who was home.

She said, "My parents are not home right now, but I can let you see the house."

"That would be great; I would like to look at it."

Eugene said, "It is a nice place and the neighborhood seems to be a nice one."

Turning to the daughter Ellen I asked, "Can you do me a favor and tell your parents to save the house for me? I really want to rent it."

She replied, "I will tell my parents."

"I am a blind person but will be going to work

starting next week. We will be back to talk with your parents so please don't rent out the house."

She replied, "Okay" and smiled.

As we drove off, my nephew said, "The house is just the right size for you."

I said, "I think that girl's parents will agree to letting me rent."

My nephew and I came back a few days later to talk with the parents. The father asked, "How are you guys doing today?"

"Fine," I replied. "I would like to rent the house, if it is okay with you. I am going to work so I need a place to live."

My nephew added, "We looked at several places and this place would be good for my uncle."

The gentleman turned to my nephew and asked, "Are you going to live here with your uncle?"

Eugene answered, "No, but I and other family members will come to check on him regularly."

"I am pretty independent and do most everything for myself from the time I wake up until bed time."

"That is great, I'll let you rent the place," said my landlord.

"Thank you very much for letting me rent," I responded. Just then the gentleman's spouse walked up.

"Our daughter Ellen said we should rent the house to the blind man."

"She must be the one who showed us the house."

"She also said that you are a nice man."

"Thank her for me. I am touched."

"We are glad to have you as our new renter."

"Great! Now I need to look for some furniture."

Eugene and I found a living room set and one small bed for a reasonable price. I was able to purchase the furniture on credit. I had done some business with this furniture store before and my credit was good. We loaded the furniture onto the truck and took it to the house I was renting. This time I had two nephews, Eugene and Stacey, helping, so we got it all set up right away. One of them said, "Hey, dude, there are no curtains for the windows."

"What about the curtain rods?" I asked.

He said, "The rods are there."

I thought I probably needed to ask my sister-in-law Bess if she could make me some more curtains. I asked, "Hey , can you measure each window?" We left and went back to Crownpoint to my older brother's house.

After coming home from work I asked my sister-in-law if she could make me some more curtains.

"Yes, all we need is the material."

Eugene said, "Here are the measurements for each window."

Bess said, "Six windows, huh? Okay, that will not be too hard."

Eugene said, "The windows are not too large."

My brother Jerry suggested "Tomorrow is Saturday so we probably can go into Gallup and get some material and other things you will need."

"That sounds good!" I was excited about going back to work again. We all went to Gallup got the material and other things I needed for the house. We took some food and cleaning items, also. My brother and his family liked where I was going to live. We went back to Crownpoint after we put everything away. My sister in-law had the curtains all ready by Sunday morning. Later that day we all left again and went to Gallup. I got all situated with the house looking pretty neat. My brother and his family had to leave so they could get ready for the new week. I said, "I will probably see you guys this weekend."

Later that evening I heard someone knocking at the front door. I opened it and it was my new landlord, Melvin. He asked, "I wanted to know if you would need a ride to work in the morning."

I replied, "Yes, that would be nice."

"Okay," he said, "I'll be here about 7:30 am."

"I'll be ready to go."

"If you need any help with anything else just holler."

"Okay I will." I went to bed later on and that first night was kind of restless.

Lying in bed, I kept thinking about my new job and how my coworkers would be towards me. I told myself I shouldn't worry as we were all supposed to work together. Finally, I fell asleep.

The next morning, I got up, drank some coffee and got ready for work. My landlord knocked on my door right at 7:30 am so I went out. He said, "Good morning, are you ready to go to work?"

I replied, "Yes, I am a little nervous, though."

He laughed and said, "You will be all right and you will get used to it sooner than you think."

"I hope so."

We drove off down the street and made it to my new work site. He instructed, "My wife or I will be here a little after 5:00 p.m. to pick you up."

I replied, "Okay; that sounds good." He helped me to get to the office front door. I walked up to the counter and said, "Good morning" to the secretary up front.

She replied, "Good morning! I will show you where your office will be."

I said, "Okay" as she took hold of my arm. We walked down a short hallway then to a fairly large office toward the back.

She explained, "I turned on the light. Your desk is over this way."

"Okay," I replied.

She described how the room was set up. "Come with me this way; I will show you the rest of the office." I and followed, her using my cane to navigate. The office was set up in a simple fashion so it was easy to navigate. The office was located in a shopping mall. This was convenient for breaks and lunch as there was a food court nearby. At first, this was good but as time went on it became expensive. Thus, I began taking my lunch.

Later in the day I talked with the other counselor Richard as he provided me with information about the program. He said, "We will take it easy at first to let you get used to this place."

I replied, "Okay I think I will do fine once I find what needs to be done."

"Great I am glad to have you here, because it has been a lot of work for one counselor and one secretary to handle." The rest of the week went slow but it was interesting. The following week, I met with the counselor and our supervisor Mr. Long to discuss clients. I was assigned 20 clients to start working with. The other counselor provided me with a list of names and addresses. I took the names and dictated a letter to my secretary, Lorie. She sent out this letter to each of my new clients and I scheduled an appointment to meet with each of them. Some of the letters were returned to our office because of an address change. I met with a few of the clients who received their letters.

The program provided services based on a manual available only in a printed format. My secretary, Lorie, read the manual cover to cover so we could record it. With the manual on tape I listened to it every chance I got to get familiar with it.

I found that it was a great tool and if I followed the contents I would do okay as a counselor. My secretary also became familiar with the manual so we could work as a team. She also recorded for me several forms that we were going to use on a regular basis. I memorized the forms that were going to be placed in each client's file folder.

By memorizing the forms when I met with each client I filled in the blanks. I recorded all information I wanted written in the blank spaces. I gave the recorded cassette tapes to my secretary to type and print. She then placed the information in each folder. This was the only method I could use because I did not have any computer skills. As time went on, working this way help me as well as my secretary to become more knowledgeable about the programs.

Lorie and I attended several trainings on the program throughout the months. Attending these training seminars and staff meetings, we met other counselors and secretaries. These individuals they offered their assistance and told us to contact them when we needed help. Knowing this and making contacts, our work performance started to become more effective. The responses we were receiving from our clients gave us an indication that we were doing well.

As time went on we developed a good sized case load with clients coming from a diverse background. There were times we accompanied our clients during their appointments for support. This increased our client level of desire and determination to do well. They often talked about the program and that we were people who cared about them.

Hearing this gave us strength and lifted our motivation to try and do more to help them.

Here, I think what help me was that I am a blind person and received similar services as a client before. Knowing this, I could understand where some of these clients were coming from and what they were going through. Each time I ran into one of my clients they seemed a little happier then when I first met them. They were always expressing their appreciation about the services they were receiving. I often told my clients that if they met the program halfway with their rehabilitation process they would be successful. Yes, there were those who left us hanging, or those who moved or got into some kind of trouble and had to leave the area.

After working for awhile I thought about purchasing a new car. I wanted a nice car so I decided on a Chevrolet Camaro. I had been saving a portion of my paycheck by joining a credit union. I thought if I didn't see the money I would not spend it. Over several months I managed to saved enough for what I thought would be a good down payment. I wanted to buy a car or have it financed somehow. I contacted the local car dealerships asking about a Chevrolet Camaro but struck out. I spoke with a sales person, Mr. Maxwell, by phone at a dealership out of town. He said, "I've got one here on the lot that is fire engine red."

"I am in Gallup," I said. "Can you save it? I will see it tomorrow."

He replied, "Okay, call first just in case before starting out." After talking to this person I contacted my younger brother, Jake Jr., in Crownpoint and told him what I wanted to do. He said, "I can take you over there tomorrow and take a look at the car." After this I went to the credit union to pick up my money that I requested earlier in the week.

Saturday morning, feeling both excited and kind of scared, I left Crownpoint headed for Aztec with Jake Jr. and his son Stacey.

We were on our way over to check out the Camaro. We got there and sure enough, it was right there on the car lot. The weird thing about this was it seemed like the car came to life. When I approached it seemed like it was waiting for me. My brother and nephew gave me a detailed description of the car. It was definitely a pretty fire engine red, with black stripes.

My nephew said, "It also has nice chrome rims."

A salesperson approached us and said, "Good morning, are you guys interested in buying this Camaro?"

"Yes," I said and asked for the salesman, Mr. Maxwell I had talked with yesterday.

He cheerfully stated, "It is your lucky day because I am that person you are looking for."

I told him that I was a blind person but wanted to buy this car.

He said, "There is no problem with that; we can talk business."

I asked, "Can we take it for a test drive?"

He responded, "Yes," and gave the car keys to my brother. The three of us got into the car and took off.

My brother said, "One time, one of my friends and I rented one of these during a rodeo in Oklahoma." The three of us kept acknowledging how great the car looked and operated. We got back to the car lot and parked the car where we picked it up.

The three of us went into an office to meet with the salesperson Mr. Maxwell. I answered all the questions the salesperson had. He asked, "Can you leave some money to hold the car for you?"

I replied, "Yes," and gave the money to my brother to hand to him.

He said, "Good; here is a receipt for you."

My brother asked, "How long do we have to wait?"

The salesperson said, "Give me three hours at the most."

My brother responded, "Okay, we will call back after we have some lunch."

"That will be fine," said the salesperson. The three of us walked out and got back into my brother's truck.

We had our lunch at a small cafe in town. After this we went over to Mother's place since it was nearby. Only our niece Karleen was at home with one of her friends. She asked, "Hey, you guys, what brings you here?"

My brother replied, "We are just cruising around." Before we got to Mother's house we all agreed not to say anything about buying a car. We got off and each of us gave her a big hug and I could picture her smiling.

My brother instructed, "Give that man a call; he should be ready by now."

I replied, "Okay," and found my way over to the phone. I dialed the number and ask for Mr. Maxwell.

He got on the phone and said, "Can I help you?"

I told him who I was and asked him about the car.

"I've got good news for you, the finance on the car has been approved."

I nervously replied, "Great; so what do I do now?"

"Come back over and sign a few more papers, and the car is yours."

When I told my brother about the good news, he said, "Good! Let's go and get it."

Just then our niece Karleen asked, "Get what?"

Jake said, "We might as well tell her."

"Tell me what?"

Turning to her my brother whispered, "Your uncle is buying a new Camaro."

She replied, "A Camaro? Wow, are you going to bring it here?"

I said, "Yes, we will let you take it for a spin."

The three of us left Mother's place and drove back to the car lot in Aztec to get the car.

Jake said, "There it is, boys. Wow, they sure shined it up."

My nephew Stacey added, "They must have washed it and parked it in front of the dealership showcase window." We walked over to the car and just then the salesmen came over.

He said, "It will be all yours as soon as you sign

the final papers, and give us the rest of the down payment."

We followed him back to his office and went over the contract. It sounded like a good deal with reasonable monthly payments. I signed the papers after my brother, as they put the car in both of our names. The reason for this was because I did not have a valid driver's license. The salesmen gave us the car keys and I proudly asked, "Who wants to drive me back to Mom's place?"

Turning towards his son, my brother said, "You can drive your uncle but be very careful."

Stacey replied, "Okay" and took hold of my arm and led me to the passenger's side. He opened the door and I got in and sat down.

He said, "Here is the seat belt" and fastened it for me.

I responded, "Wow, let's cruise!" He came around and got in from the driver's side.

He said, "Man, this is a nice car!" My brother pulled alongside us and stated, "I will follow you guys."

We started down the street that led to the main highway. As we took off, on the main highway, I felt the power in this car.

We drove over to Mom's place which was about 15 miles away. We pulled up onto the driveway just as my niece Karleen came out.

She said, "Wow, that is a pretty car!"

I got out and asked, "Do you want to take it for a cruise now?"

"I don't know, because it looks pretty fast."

My brother laughed and said, "Come on; I'll go with you." Just then another nephew, Jackson, drove up and parked his truck.

He came over and asked, "Whose new ride is it?"

My brother said, "Your uncle just bought it a while ago and we barely got here."

Jackson suggested, "Let's take it for a cruise."

Jake replied, "You guys go ahead and go and I will wait here for Mother." My nephew Stacey and I got in the back seat and let Jackson and Karleen sit in the front.

Jackson said "Let me drive it first."

My niece replied, "Go ahead, because I am kind of scared."

We took off and drove over to Farmington, about 20 miles away. As we drove around in the mall parking lot some of my nephew's friends saw him. They yelled out at him to stop so he did. One of them said, "Nice car, is this your new ride?"

He replied humorously, "Yes, do you like it?"

Another one of them said, "Yeah, it's a nice car, and it sounds pretty neat."

My nephew Jackson said, "Yeah, and it has a V-8 instead of a V-6 engine."

Another one asked, "When did you get it?"

My nephew answered, "I was just kidding around; it isn't mine. My uncle from Gallup just bought it." After cruising around for a while we took off back to Mom's place. We pulled up to the driveway and my brother; Mom and sister Cynthia came out to see the car. My brother volunteered to take them for a ride. Everyone liked the new car. Teasingly, they asked, "When can I borrow it for a weekend?" I did not say anything – just stood there smiling.

Later on the three of us left Mom's place and started following each other. This time my brother drove the new car through town until we got way out of Farmington. After this, he let his son drive me back to Crownpoint. He instructed, "Take it easy, because the car needs to be broken in for several more miles."

We replied, "Okay" and started off for Crownpoint as my brother followed us.

My nephew said, "I sure like your new car and I was the first one to drive it."

I jokingly replied, "Later on maybe I can get the chance to drive it."

"That would really be great."

"Yeah, I am only kidding," I admitted.

"Someday I will have one like this," he said.

"One time, your uncle Jerry's friend Tom left his Camaro at the house for about a week."

"Really?"

"Yes, and I told your cousin Eugene that one day I would have one of my own."

He responded, "Yeah, and now you have one."

I said proudly, "Yes, I hope to keep it for a long time." After cruising for a while we drove back into Crownpoint. When we got back to my brother's house, we pulled up to the driveway. My sister-in-law Berta came out and said, "Wow, you guys got a pretty car!"

I responded, "Yeah, we did."

My brother asked, "Do you want to go for a ride?"

"Yes, I do." My nephew and I went inside as they drove off. Later, I had my nephew take me back to my older brother's place where I usually stayed. I told my nephew I would give him a call in the morning to have him bring the car over.

He said, "Okay" and drove off.

There was no one home at Jerry's place, so I went inside and waited. The family came home later that night. I did not mention anything about the car and went to bed later.

The next morning around mid-morning I gave my nephew Stacey a call and asked, "Can you bring the car over now?"

"Okay. When I get there I will blow the horn." When he came, we heard a car horn and there was a red car outside.

Jerry said, "Someone is outside in a new red car." He started out the door and poked his head back inside to tell us who it was. I played it cool and followed the family outside. Just then, my nephew Eugene asked, "Is this your new car?"

I proudly replied, "Yes, we bought it yesterday."

Joey, Gracie, Mom, Etta, Cindy

My brother asked, "Who wants to go for a ride with me?"

My sister-in-law responded, "I do," and two of my nieces got in and they drove off. When they came back my two nephews, Eugene and Stacey, took off to go for a cruise. My brother turned to me and said, "You got a nice car."

I replied, "Thanks" and we shook hands which is a traditional gesture. When the boys came back, they opened up the car hood to take a look at the engine. My nephew Eugene said, "This is a nice car with a lot of horsepower."

As we were looking, he described what all was under the hood. Jerry came up to us and asked, "What are you guys doing?"

My nephew Eugene replied, "I am describing the engine to my uncle."

My brother looked at it and said, "No wonder the car has a lot of power." After everybody took a ride, my nephew Eugene and I took my other nephew Stacey, back to his house. I told my younger brother Jake Jr. "I will keep the car up at our brother's place for the time being.

He said, "Okay, if you want to keep it here, it will be okay."

I humorously responded, "I might take it back to Gallup where I live."

My nephew and nieces took me back to Gallup later in the evening so I could go to work in the morning. Before I left Crownpoint I asked if anyone would be available to bring the car over around noon time on Friday.

My nephew Eugene asked, "What do you need?"

I replied, "I have some money left and I would like to

have the windows tinted."

He stated, "That would look real neat."

Just then my sister-in-law Bess said, "I can probably bring the car over on Friday."

I answered, "I will make an appointment for the tint and get off from work at noon." Friday came around to have the car windows tinted which turned out looking pretty sharp. Eventually, the car became my nephew Eugene's car as he drove it most of the time. I would call him when I needed to go somewhere out of town. The car was very reliable as it took us anywhere we wanted to go. The whole family had their chance to use the car. I remember we had the car for only a couple of weeks and someone keyed it along the side from front to back. When I found out I confidently stated, "That is okay, it only means that the car will last for a long time."

I worked for this agency for about three years and had my ups and downs with clients and staff members. I worked with three different secretaries and for several months between secretary vacancies I worked alone. During these times I dictated all my work on cassette tapes. My supervisor brought a couple of secretaries from the main office to help me for a couple of days twice a month. This way I was able to keep up with the demands of the job. There were many times my clients offered their help, but because of confidentiality issues, I did not accept. For personal reasons, I made a decision to resign from my position. There were many occasions where I came across my former clients who often asked me to come back to work.

Next I started working for the independent living program located in Aztec. Here I helped individuals with a disability residing in their own homes utilizing the four core services. The four core skills included providing advocacy, independent living skills training, peer support, and information and referral sources. The mission was to help these individuals learn and utilize these core skills to live somewhat independently.

First, I started working as a peer support mentor. I visited individuals living with a disability at their homes. During the first visit with these individuals we provided general information about the program. If the person was interested we scheduled a time to come back and start the initial paperwork. For a couple of months there were a few of us with a disability doing this. I could almost feel what some of these individuals were going through as I had flashbacks about when I first became blind.

When I provided peer mentorship, I listen to what was being said most of the time. Sometimes I sat with them and hardly spoke a word. There were times we would have a good conversation and laugh. Other times just before an appointment the new clients would call the center to cancel. During the first few days of visiting I had to earn their trust which was the core of peer mentorship. After doing so we connected and the conversation became more relaxed. When this portion was in play the clients would start asking me about my blindness. The first thing I would tell them is to close their eyes real tight. This would give them a good sign of my current vision. I tried not to talk about me so much because I was there to help them.

I can recall when the staff met in a one-room donated office with one telephone. When the phone rang we almost jumped at the same time to answer it.

One day after doing this for a while sitting around a table our boss, Shirley, came in. She said, "Guess what, guys?"

Looking toward her we asked, "What is it?"

She responded, "We finally got some good news."

Bernice, one of the other ladies asked, "What are you talking about?"

Shirley replied, "We were awarded a grant for operational costs."

We all exclaimed, "A grant? That is great!"

She informed us, "Now I will put out job announcements for some positions."

I replied, "Some positions, huh?"

She responded, "Yes, I encourage you guys to apply when they come out." The job announcements came out so I applied for one of the independent living specialist positions. I continued to provide peer mentorship and one day I was called for an interview. I made the interview and after some time I was offered the position, which I accepted and started working full time.

Together with the other independent living specialist and a couple of peer mentors, we had our planning meetings as to how we were going to work.

While working here the staff and clients went on a ski trip into Colorado. The ski resort had an adaptive sports program utilizing volunteers. They were able to accommodate individuals with a physical or mental disability. I got a chance to go skiing with the group to Colorado. I tried skiing as a blind person once before with a friend April while living down in Alamogordo. I really did not get the hang of balancing myself so the skis were sliding everywhere. With the same friend I also tried ice skating on the next day. This was even more difficult as I was unable to remain standing up.

We arrived at the ski resort and everybody was ready to go. I met up with my instructors as I was assigned two people, Candy and Chris. I was fitted with ski boots which felt weird as I went walking around in the ski lodge. My instructors and I went outside so I could put on my skis and start receiving instructions. Here I realized that there were many ways to control how a person skis. All morning long when I was getting off the ski lift I fell backwards. I finally asked my boss, Shirley, to describe what the place looked like where people got off the lift. She describe it in detail, and after planting this description in my mind I did not fall backwards any more. I went on several more ski trips with the staff and clients. Each time I improved my skiing skills. I told my nephew Eugene and nieces Shaw, Jerrileen and Yvonne about the ski trip.

I guess I encouraged them to try it. I went skiing with them several times and even our little granddaughter Rylee enjoyed skiing. I don't remember how old she was but she did well with help from her dad. Afterwards, on our way home while eating dinner we talked and laughed about our experiences. The next day most of us had some muscle soreness but it was a good sore.

My next job brought me back to Gallup. I was selected to coordinate the Gallup satellite office. I started program operations from donated office space with one desk, one chair and my computer. I was able to perform work duties and kept track of things on my computer. I worked alone for several months until we were able to hire Janelle, a peer mentor, and Irene, an independent living specialist. These individuals started as part time workers. Part of my duties was to train these two individuals as we worked together.

As a team, we worked out of the donated office for several months. In the meantime I checked out several places for office space. There were several places available but they were not accessible for people using a wheelchair. I finally found a place where we started with an empty room. As time went on some office furniture was donated by other programs. We managed to put together a nice looking office.

One day I made up my mind to seriously abstain from alcohol use after drinking off and on. I got myself physically sick by drinking to extremes and suffered the consequences in the hospital. I owe countless thanks to my nephew Eugene and my younger brother, Jake Jr., for being there when it really counted. I came to a point where if I kept on drinking I would eventually die from alcohol poisoning. I did not want to die so I worked extra hard to start on the road of recovery.

Somewhere deep in my mind I found the strength to come back to reality. I really don't know what took place but getting away from alcohol was the best thing to happen to me. The rest of the family and friends provided their neverending support.

Abstaining from alcohol use gave me more determination and positive energy to continue to help those struggling. I had a better approach doing my job at the center with less stress. We primarily provided the same four core services we did at our main center. We held monthly support group meetings at our center.

I usually let the clients decide what to discuss or do during the meetings. Usually the discussions went on for a while then we played games to win prizes that were donated by staff and clients.

We put together several potluck dinners at our center. We also went on several outings to have a cookout. I let the clients make the choices because it was a client-directed center.

I got a group of my clients interested in going skiing up in Colorado where I went before. We also went river rafting in the same area in Colorado. We did our own fund raising events to make enough money to pay for the skiing and rafting trip. Some staff members volunteered to use their vehicles and gas to make this event a success. I always kept in mind that I was doing this for the clients. There were many times I worked overtime just to help these individuals.

During my employment with the independent living center I attended several seminars and conferences. I traveled throughout the Navajo reservation and surrounding states to attend these events. I was part of the audience or sometimes I was one of the presenters at these events.

The majority of these events addressed disability awareness and gave inspiration to the clients and the public. The furthest I traveled to attend a conference was going to Washington D. C. with my coworker and good friend Janelle. We traveled by plane to get there and back. We boarded the plane from Albuquerque and returned there. I met several Native Americans with other disabilities from different Indian Nations. I was invited to attend this conference as one of the presenters. After the conference was over I remember getting in a cab at the hotel headed for the airport. The taxi driver asked me what my name was so I told him.

He said sincerely, "I like your last name so I want to do something with it."

I asked, "What are you talking about?"

He responded, "I want to rename the international airport here using your name."

Talking about conferences, I remember while in Gallup I and my coworker Janelle put together one of these disability awareness conferences. It took a lot of hard work and time to do it. It was only the two of us operating the program at the time so we had to go at it alone. The thing here is that we were able to pull it off, and with the feedback we received from other programs, it was all worth it. I was in front of the audience running the conference all day. I was able to keep on schedule because I made my agenda in Braille. My coworker, Janelle, was out in front taking care of registration and giving out information. Some of our clients volunteered their time to help. Some of them also participated in the conference by speaking on a panel. I remember afterwards I learned we'd had a good turnout from the public.

One day, some of the staff members along with our main boss came down from the main center. We were told that we no longer had a job, because we were all being laid off. The time I was here I was able to help many individuals to be able to help themselves. Many times I was approached by these individuals to tell me that I inspired them to do more for themselves

Chapter Ten
Graduate Program and Licensure

One day I started taking classes at the local Western New Mexico University Graduate Study Center. I thought of trying for a master's degree in counseling at this campus. I had been out of work for over a year since being laid off. It was convenient for me at the time to take classes. There was an express bus that would take me to class and afterwards I could use the taxi to return home. I thought this way I could increase my level of education and continue to help people help themselves.

When I enrolled at WNMU I did so feeling more confident. I had more skills approaching college as a blind person than I had previously. After class began, I quickly found out that to complete this journey successfully I would have to work twice as hard as the sighted students. This was not like undergrad work as this was more specific and detailed. Only an A or B grade meant anything during this task. This meant keeping up with reading, term papers and all assignments.

Another thing I had to learn quickly was the layout of the building. I needed to know my way around the building both outside and inside. I had to learn where each classroom and other rooms were located. To get by for the time being, my a good friend and coworker Janelle helped me.

We worked together at the independent living center so she was familiar with helping blind people. She knew what to look for and how to describe it to me. Again, using her descriptions, I placed that image in my mind like I did many times before in these kinds of situations. At this point in my blindness it was taking place almost automatically when someone described something to me. After learning the architectural structure of the campus I developed a photographic map in my mind as to how the building was laid out. I found where each class room was located, where the stairs and other permanent objects were. There were no Braille markings or raised lettering on the classroom doors or the framework around the doors for identification purposes. The only places that had Braille labeling were the bathrooms. This issue was brought to the administration's attention. The missing Braille markings and raised lettering were placed on order and shortly afterward were put where they belonged. After the signs and labels were in their proper places, making it easier to maneuver in the building. I would imagine that the next blind or visually-impaired person will have it a little easier while taking classes at this campus.

Another thing I had them do was install screen reader software in one of the computers. This allowed me to take some of the exams myself using the computer.

The new accessibility provided security so I would not feel left out when we worked in the computer lab. This gave me a little more independence and confidence. As a blind person, I learned that however small, a newly learned skill still improves my ability to be independent.

The other thing I recognized quickly was that the professors and office staff had little or no experience in working with visually impaired students. I was able to work together with the professors and other staff members on campus as time went on.

Each semester was a good challenge for me. What I learned was to keep up with all reading and homework assignments. I pushed myself and work twice as hard as the other students to make sure I got the grade I wanted. At first I was kind of quiet until I got to know some of the students and professors better. I started participating more each time I had a new class. I had computer skills so I did the majority of my work myself. During one of my first classes I began to work with a reader named Liz. We worked well together and she and I became good friends. I also had another reader, Kay, with whom worked well and became good friends. My readers helped me where I needed some visual assistance like proofreading my term papers. They also helped me get to class or back home after class. There were other students who helped when my readers were busy.

I think this whole thing at this campus was a learning experience for both the staff and students. One day a professor, Dr. Mason, and I decided to conduct a classroom activity. The purpose of this activity was to find out how much trust we had. I brought some bandanas to use as blindfolds and had the students pair off in twos. One of them put on a blindfold while the other one guided them around.

I remember some of the students stated that it was difficult to move even a little way. I think they got a good idea of what I go through on a daily basis.

When it came time, I was eligible to graduate with the rest of the class. I successfully passed all course requirements with a favorable GPA and also passed the exit exam. My family members who could make it to my graduation were present. My nephew Eugene escorted me again to get my diploma. After graduation, the family all went over to my mobile home. We all decided to go out and have some Mexican food at one of my favorite places. I changed my clothes and put on the ones I usually wore, like casual western wear. My younger sister Cynthia teasingly said, "Now you look like the rest of us."

I replied, "Yeah," then laughed. I remember my mother stated, "This graduation was different from the ones I have attended."

Teasingly I responded, "It is because this was a real graduation, Mom."

I did my internship at an inpatient alcohol treatment center and picked up a good amount of hands-on counseling experience there. I also did some outpatient counseling during this time. I thought I was ready to go to work to do some serious counseling to help people. I applied for employment with several agencies where a counselor's position was open. When I went for the job interviews they asked me if I were state licensed. My response was that I did not have a license. After checking into this licensing thing, I found out that I had to jump through several hoops even before being considered to take the NCE – National Counselors Exam. Times like this I actually felt my blindness, but somehow maintained my composure. I think this comes from what my dad shared with me one day.

He advised me, "If you want something good out of life you will have to work hard to get it because it will not be easy." Another thing that comes to mind during these I call hard times is this:

While in the hospital a female person appeared beside my bed stating, "You should go back to school; you can become what ever you want to be, because you are a bright person." I remember this was all she said and disappeared from the room. I tried talking back to her but she was not there. This made me wonder if it was a real person there at the time.

I manage to get all necessary documents to their proper place to apply for state licensure. I was scheduled to take the NCE but fell short on my first attempt. I took the first exam for granted, thinking that with a masters, I would have no problem passing it. After receiving and reviewing my exam results I approached the NCE with a different concept. My preparation for the next exam took a good amount of research and backtracking. I put together a study guide about counseling that I typed on my computer. I reviewed the study guide as often as I could, concentrating on my weak points.

I was ready to retake the exam so I left a day early and spent the night near the testing site. I got up early the next morning and had a good breakfast with a couple of friends, Kara and Simon, who drove me over. The three of us arrived at the testing site and went inside. I reported in like before with the person in charge. He said, "You can go in and start taking the exam now."

I replied, "Okay, where is my reader, to read the exam?"

He responded, "What reader? I don't know anything about that."

I stated, "I informed the testing agency that I would need a reader to read the exam to me as one of the accommodations."

He replied, "Hold on; let me call them." The three of us sat in the front room waiting for him. He returned, approached my friend Kara and asked, "Can you read the exam for him?"

She responded, "Yes, I think I can."

He paused. "Let me ask the agency if it will be okay to do that."

She said, "Okay, I'll wait." I started feeling sort of upset because someone goofed up when I was good and ready. He returned and explained, "The agency cannot accept you to do the reading, because they have their own readers." I thought to myself, *if they have their own readers then why don't we have one here today?* Eventually the exam had to be rescheduled until a reader was definitely in place. I spoke with one of the exam personnel staff, trying to find out what happened.

I received the new date to take the exam so I made arrangements with my friend Simon. This time only two of us made the trip from Gallup. After arriving there we had some difficulty with the reader situation again.

This time the result was more in our favor. During my exam I had an excellent reader, Shelly, reading the exam. I took a different approach when I took the exam. Here I had the reader read the questions forward and backward. I also had her do the same with the multiple choice answers. We also split the question in half and read the second half first. This way I had a better understanding of the questions. Being a blind person, I was allowed additional time to complete the exam. I completed the exam in the time allowed with a couple of minutes to spare. Sitting there, both of us exhausted from the exam, I heard a knock on the door. The door opened up and it was the person monitoring the exam. She excitedly stated, "You passed the exam."

I replied, "That is great."

She spoke again, "That was a very difficult exam you took."

By this time it didn't matter to me if the exam was any more difficult because I passed it. I thanked the person who read the exam and asked, "If it is okay with you, can I recommend you to read for others?"

She confidently replied, "Yes, that will be fine with me."

I assured her, "Having a good reader with patience makes all the difference."

A few weeks went by and I had not heard from the licensing department. I thought I had better check up on my counseling license. I called the license department and they told me that I did not show up to take the exam. This got me sort of upset so I started calling and sending e-mail messages to the responsible agencies. After spending about a month cleaning up the mess, I received my state counseling license.

Finally I was now a licensed mental health counselor! With this new leverage I thought I would be able to land a good job in the counseling field.

Chapter Eleven
Life Goes On

Sitting here in my mobile home, I sometimes take a mental trip back to the houses I lived in during my childhood. This usually happens when an event reminds me of how things were when I had my vision. I will never forget the good times I spent with my family and many close friends living in Crownpoint.

Being blind for several years, I have learned to be self-sufficient and independent. This was a long and hard fight, yet an adventurous journey. I am aware of the daily risks involved in being blind but try to push this thought aside quickly. I take care of my daily living activities from the time I wake up until bedtime. Each day I take care of what needs attention on a daily basis. I try take care of needs as they arise, not procrastinate. I learned to keep my things arranged in order so I would know where things are in my mobile home. My family and friends respect this for my safety. For example, one of my nieces or my nephew Eugene lets me know that things are in order before leaving. Each day is always different as some days are a drag and other days are nice.

To do my cooking sometimes I use a skillet or pan on top of the stove. I use the oven a lot to bake or roast my meats. One Christmas my nephew Eugene bought me a medium-sized indoor electric grill to cook other meats. I like to cook steaks, hamburgers, pork chops and other meats on my grill. I also use a crockpot to slowcook different kinds of stew or chili beans. I love to make hot salsa with fresh ingredients and have it with chips. Some of my friends like my salsa so when they want some I would make it for them. I usually cook something I feel like eating.

I have a Medtronic device to set cooking time when I use the electric grill. For example, I would grill meat for ten minutes so I set the timer. Other times I use my talking clock or watch to keep track of cooking time.

These electronic devices have a build-in electronic voice. I use a microwave oven to reheat left over food or heat up microwaveable goodies. There are times I pay more attention to the smell of the meat cooking – that lets me know it is done.

A couple of times a year, I invite family members and some friends over to have a potluck dinner at my place. I make sure they are not planned on special holidays or birthdays. I would send out a menu by e-mail to my nephew Eugene and nieces Shawmarie, Jerrileen and Yvonne. This way they would have a good idea of what to bring. Each of us has our favorite dish we prepare. My older brother Jerry or someone cooks the steaks, burgers and hot dogs for us. Each time, I invite family members or friends, but some of them don't show up. I would think to myself that is okay because that leaves more food for the rest of us.

Kylee, Rylee, Ty-Jordan, Shawmarie, and DeJong DeGroat

My older brother was blessed with two granddaughters, Rylee and Kylee, and a grandson Ty-Jordan. I and others always have a ball with them at our potlucks. My nieces and nephew come by to visit when they have the time. Otherwise we keep in touch by phone or e-mail. I also talk a lot with our three little grand kids by phone or they come by to visit. I have several other nieces and nephews living here and there. The ones I mention a lot are the ones who have spent more time with me. My nieces and nephew graduated from high school and have attended post high school education to pursue a degree. Some of them are working and taking classes at the same time. They are all living on their own and providing for themselves. Eventually one day they, too, may achieve their master's degree as I have confidence in them. I feel that I have left all my nieces and nephew with a good amount of inspiration to continue with their education.

Getting around town I use the express bus during the weekdays. I use it to go to the post office, the bank, the hospital, downtown or to the mall. I learned where the bus stops are located so when I use the bus I know where to start and conclude. I usually walk to the nearby stores and fast food places using my white cane. Sometimes I feel like taking a long walk so I take off down the sidewalk. Before learning some of these independent living skills I was unable to go walking alone. The times I don't go walking are when it is too windy, at night or when there is snow on the side walks. I had a few close calls when I was crossing at a busy intersection. I almost got hit by a car when someone came around the corner unexpectedly just as I was starting to cross. A couple of times they ran over the tip of my cane and they just kept on going. This upset me and frightened me a little. I learned that the best thing to do is forget what just happened right away. This way it does not hang around in my mind and create fear in me.

To go grocery shopping I usually go with a relative from back home usually a niece, a nephew, or a family member. I would type out a shopping list for groceries and household needs on my computer. I learned that using a shopping list made it easier for whoever was helping me that day. I remember once my friend Kara said, "You made your shopping list with each item listed in its section according to the isles in the store." If family members are not available, I would call one of my friends here in town to take me. I have a couple, Kara and Simon, who I became close friends with so we help one another. Whoever is helping me also helps me to go and pay for monthly bills.

There are times I did not have anyone around to help me. I thought to myself, if I wanted to get it done, I would need to get out there and do it myself. I would get myself ready and catch the express bus downtown to the bank.

I would start from there and go here and there by bus and do a lot of walking. I would do this for a couple of days to complete the task. I would feel great that I was capable of doing it alone. Other times with someone either a relative or a close friend we would use my pickup truck to do these chores. When I have to go out of town I would use my truck with a driver. I hardily used a transits bus for quite some time because of using my truck. Today there are times I need to go somewhere out of town so I catch the transits bus or the train. It feels great to use other transportation methods and not having to depend on someone to drive me. Sometimes, I would get on the city express bus near my trailer and get off downtown and walk over to one of the restaurants to.

I have been seeking full or part time employment in the counseling field as a licensed counselor. I am trying to establish employment here in the local area so I don't have to relocate again. I would apply for counseling jobs that are advertised, but have been hitting dead ends again. After applying I would anticipate promising things from some programs but none. In the mean time

I do volunteer work here and there helping individuals going through some form of crisis. I also started doing motivational speeches that I enjoy doing. I want to continue these motivational speeches especially to the young people. Many times I received a call from a friend seeking some form of help. Sometimes they would come over and through talking they end up helping themselves. The majority of the time I do more listening then talking.

For entertainment, I enjoy going skiing with my nephew Eugene and nieces Yvonne and Jerrileen and granddaughter Rylee in Colorado. We try to at least go up one time during each ski season. I do my skiing with the assistance of one or two instructors.

These instructors are volunteers with many years of experience skiing with individuals who are blind. When I go skiing I picture the slope trails as though as if I was driving on a snow packed highway. One day I would like to try snow boarding where I go skiing. During the early Summer I enjoy going to California to ride the giant roller coasters with my nieces Shawmarie, Jerrileen and Yvonne and nephew Eugene. We started doing this when my nieces and nephew were still in high school. We would pack up our bags and take off as soon as school let out for the summer. We been to California several times over the years to get away from home. I think I enjoy these activities because I get a chance to feel the physical effects. I can still feel the coasters slowly chugging there way upwards and stopping momentarily when it reaches the top. My nieces and nephew would tell me how high we are when we reach the very top of the tracks. I can still hear people, starting to scream even before the coaster takes off downwards. Getting off the coaster after the ride I would be kind of wobbly when I walked. Each of us would tell about how each of us felt during the ride.

I listen to high school, college and professional sports being broadcast over the radio. I like this because they are done in play by play action. Just recently they have been doing some of the sports in my Native Navajo language. These are high school, college or professional sports like basketball or football games. With all the modern technology available they are done over the internet that I sometime use. I remember I only had a small radio powered by flash light batteries for listening.

I had no other choice, being without utilities sitting at my dad's house back at Standing Rock. Today, I have different electronic devices to use for leisure enjoyment. I enjoy listening to music of different types and watching a movie now and then.

I did mention something about my computer skill earlier in the book. With a pointer here and there from different individuals I learned how to navigate the computer. This computer is provided by the state's blind services program. It is just like any other computer except this one is equipped with a software screen reader. This means that the software recognizes what's on the screen at that point and time. After, it recognizes it then the computer voice reads it aloud through external speakers. Another thing is whichever key you press on the keyboard the computer voice lets you know. This allows me to stay on track where I am on the computer. As a blind person I do not have access to using the mouse like sighted people. I learn how to use the keyboard to navigate my way around the computer. Some where along the line I found a way to use the keyboard to function like using a mouse. With my computer I have access in reading personal mail using a scanner. This way I am able to be aware of what or how much I need to pay for each account. With the computer I have access to many different things that sighted people have. I am thankful that someone came out with such a product like the screen reader so I won't be left in the dark. I feel that I am ambitious, so I am going to continue to learn more about the computer. I provide training to other individuals who are blind. I teach them how to navigate the computer using the keyboard and a screen reader.

Today I keep in touch with family and friends by telephone, cellular phone or e-mail.

I remember after a few months of Braille training I was able to write letters again using Braille. Unknowingly this increased my level of independence to communicate back then. I recall one day when the kids were small I got a Braille letter from a friend. I was reading it when I started laughing about something she wrote.

My nieces and nephew curiously asked, "What are you laughing about?" I told them I was reading my Braille letter and my friend Barb told me something funny. I also recall when working for the independent living center one of our clients received a Braille letter from China. Early in his blindness, he did not know how to read Braille yet so they asked me to interpret. I got the Braille letter and translated it by typing it on my computer then putting it on a floppy disc. This way he was able to read it on his computer. I feel fortunate that I am able to read and write Braille. I continue to use Braille to label certain items I use on a daily bases or for marking my clothes. I taught Shawmarie one of my nieces how to read enough Braille so she could help me label my clothes using a needle and thread. Another interesting communication technique I experienced while working was communicating with a deaf person. We did this with the assistance of a relay operator. Now I think I will be able to communicate with most any one with the use of e-mail. Just the other day one of my friends, Janelle, said, "I will be getting internet services so we can e-mail one another."

When I first became blind I felt helpless, frightened, angry and thought of being punished. Over the years there are many times I felt like giving up because of struggling day after day. Tired of this craziness, there were times that I went through suicidal ideations. When this occurred I manage to pull my thoughts back together.

I was able to do this by thinking about what would happen to my family if I were to carry out that stupid idea. Other times, I would get frustrated, especially when someone stood me up, and never told me why it happened. I guess this was because they were the ones who would make the suggestion of doing something together. I had to make up my mind to move forward or remain helpless at home. I thought to myself that there are only two ways to go.

The two ways are, either getting it done or don't do it at all, because there is no in between. I often said to myself, "Get tough or die." I also used this term on some of my friends who were experiencing some form of difficulty. I still remember how some people treated me because I was blind. I think they felt that all blind people are the same – helpless. I remember when people talked to me they would raise their voices as though I had a hearing problem. Other times they would talk directly to the person I was with instead of at me. One time one of my younger brother's Jake Jr. stated directly, "You can ask the man, he is standing right here," to a sales clerk. I was able to overcome many obstacles and challenges I faced and from what society tossed out.

By doing so I have inspired many individuals who were faced with challenges to move on. Today I feel that in spite of what happens to us we can adapt and make the necessary adjustments to be successful in life. I also feel that may be my reason for becoming blind is that one day I would be helping other people who may be struggling. Sometimes all we need is for someone to hear what we have to say.

Reaching this level of significance in my journey, I thought I might mention what my ultimate goal is. I hope one day to achieve a PhD in psychology to become a psychologist. I am thinking about integrating my Navajo traditional learning with the psychology of the Western.

Throughout my years as a blind person I trained my hearing to guide me. I learned to use it in practically everything I did or attempted to do. When I would hear something, my training automatically planted a picture in my mind what the noise might look like.

When someone describes something to me then I can picture it and remember it for a long time. With my hearing and memory, I am able to function as though I am not blind. Many times I have been told that I function like I can see or did not act like a blind person. Today I can look in the direction the noise came from and almost describe what it would look like just by hearing. Having my vision before also helps me when it comes to visualization of something I hear. With the unique way I was able to train my hearing and mind to work together effectively, I thought of giving this unique title to my book: *My Hearing and Memory Become My Vision*. To me this title makes sense as I mentioned several times through out the book that my hearing and memory are what guide me. I anticipate this will continue to be true for a long time. However, my final title choice, *Blindness Should Not Be a Burden*, is intended to encourage other individuals with some level of visual impairment that they can succeed in spite of it.